Commendations

In front of me is a volume of sermons. Sermons which were given from life and for life. Whoever knows Marcel Rebiai knows that he is a man who's not just interested in words for words' sake, but it is important for him to speak a "word." A word of the living God. So in his sermons we sense the listening. Listening to the God who speaks. The sermon style is retained in the book. However – here no one is preaching to me, but it is as if Marcel were sitting on a bench with me and we were studying the Bible text together. Questions are asked, the meanings of words are pored over and parallel texts are considered.

Aspects of personal spiritual counseling often arise. Questions which concern my spiritual life, questions which animate me. The book of sermons becomes a conversation between friends and God. Marcel Rebiai brings no dry commentary, but enters into the Scriptures with his own life. This is a typically Hebrew or Jewish way to reflect on the Bible. Not that I "reflect" on the word from the outside, but the word illuminates my life from all sides.

The author poses questions asked by everyone who seriously wants to be a Christian. Doubt, fear, guilt and sin are not excluded. And he speaks openly about the things that rankle. But always in a way that does not jar, causing me to close up, but a way which helps me become open for Jesus' healing and helping word.

Friedhelm Geiss, Berlin

Marcel Rebiai's new book *In God's Image* is a devotional "must-read" for all who are serious about their spiritual lives. It is filled with scriptural insights, yet always sensitive to the "Everyman" (and Everywoman) seeker in our midst, for whom Christ is not yet a clear reality. As one progresses through the book, however, more and more the implications of following the "real Jesus" become clearer and stronger, more practical and more demanding/ inviting, with every page.

Reminiscent of the practical spirituality of Corrie ten Boom and Watchman Nee of a previous generation, this book both amazes and delights, brings consternation and joy, and breathes into the reader himself/herself something of the atmosphere in which it was written. I cannot recommend this book enough to those whose ears and heart are open to what the Spirit is saying to God's people today.

Dr Lance Wonders,
Dean of Acts Bible College, Minnesota, USA

In God's Image has the capacity to draw the true disciple to the master. This small but valuable book contains messages that reflect Marcel's own faith journey – a journey that speaks of an intimate relationship with God the Father. His simple approach to the Scriptures belies a depth of theological understanding that is so helpful to the non-academic seeking a similar walk with God. The book will also be a valuable text for anyone engaged in helping others grasp both the beauty and the cost of being a true and faithful disciple of Jesus the Messiah. Thank you, Marcel, for this godly contribution – well done, good and faithful servant!

Evan Thomas, Israel

Marcel Rebiai speaks from his heart in an outspoken, profound, passionate and yet reflected way. He does not endeavor to conform God's Word to our time, but to return to the very essence of the message of Jesus Christ. Marcel Rebiai's volume of sermons is in a sense a basic course of faith for people who want to adopt for their lives the riches that are in Christ Jesus.

Martin Buehlmann,
Director of Vineyard Ministries, Dach, Europe

With his exposition Marcel Rebiai proves that he has gained deep insight into spiritual connections, as well as into the processes, deviations and aberrations of the human soul.

Wolfhard Margies,
Senior Pastor of Gemeinde auf dem Weg,
Berlin, Germany

I like the authenticity without glamour and without a claim to the absolute truth – but with a deep commitment.

Lorenz Reithmeier, Executive Director of the
Spiritual Renewal Movement in Germany

In God's Image

Marcel Rebiai

Sovereign World

Sovereign World Ltd
PO Box 784
Ellel
Lancaster LA1 9DA
England

www.sovereignworld.com

Translated from German by Susan Wiesmann.

The original German edition *Im Bilde Gottes* was published © 2008 by
SCM R. Brockhaus, SCM-Verlag GmbH & Co. KG, Witten, Germany.

ISBN: 978-1-85240-535-9

The publishers aim to produce books which will help to extend and build up the Kingdom of God. We do not necessarily agree with every view expressed by the authors,
or with every interpretation of Scripture expressed. We expect readers to make their
own judgment in the light of their understanding of God's Word and in an attitude of
Christian love and fellowship.

Cover design by ThirteenFour Design
Typeset by **documen**, www.documen.co.uk
Printed in the United Kingdom

Dedicated to my wife Regula,
to my children Elija, Ephraim,
Immanuel, Hanna, Stefan,
and to all my brothers and sisters
in the Community of Reconciliation.

Contents

Contents

FOREWORD BY COLIN URQUHART

The Christian life is about relationship with God through Jesus Christ, in a daily walk with Him, in the person of the Holy Spirit, in relationship with other believers and with those who belong to the world. True disciples take all these aspects of relationship seriously.

Relationships take time to build. They do not happen through reading about the kind of relationships we ought to have as believers. They are the result of applying the gospel, God's Word, to every area of our lives.

Marcel Rebiai helps the reader to do just that, and so strengthen and deepen his or her relationships as a result. Divided into manageable sections to be used on a daily basis, the reader has time to assimilate the revelation of truth given for each day, and the time to process these truths so that they find substance in his or her life.

Speaking from thorough knowledge of the Scriptures and from years of practical application in close relationship with other believers, the author is well equipped to lead the reader though a developing revelation of the truth in a way that will enable him or her to live in the glorious freedom Christ has made possible for His followers. They can be faithful witnesses by bearing fruit for God's glory.

These are the aims of the Christian life, and this book will enable any serious reader to see these aims outworked in his or her life.

Prayer

Glowing flame
which penetrates my heart
melt out
all the trifles, all the trash
Shell out
the little which is true
So that the true light will shine
Then grace
with its healing hands
can move in me
And the mustard seed will grow after all

Elija Rebiai

FOREWORD BY ELIJA REBIAI

When we consider Jesus and His work we notice that He had many followers but only a few disciples. When He multiplied bread and fish for His listeners, there were five thousand men with Him, not counting the women and children. But when He sent out His disciples in pairs, there were only seventy-two. What, then, is the difference between a normal follower and a disciple? A disciple is an active follower of a teacher and his teaching; a disciple is someone's pupil. A disciple strives to become like his master. Jesus said His disciple would follow after Him. "Whoever wants to be my disciple must deny themselves and...follow me" (Matthew 16:24 TNIV).

Why didn't the masses follow after Jesus? They listened to Him but remained passive listeners, consumers. Only a fraction of them were real disciples. The problem was that it was not humanly possible to carry out Jesus' teaching and the path He took. Nothing could be proven, nothing explained with common sense. How could someone say that His disciple must deny himself and take his cross on himself and simultaneously claim, "My yoke is easy and My burden light"? How could someone who went around as an outcast also prepare heavenly dwellings for His disciples? Jesus' demands were radical and impossible to fulfill. The only way to relate with Him was to believe Him. Belief without any guarantee and against all logic.

Deciding to accept Jesus' salvation today is also a step of faith but (in our culture) poses little risk. It does not cost much to become a Christian, merely the honesty and humility to admit one's own sinfulness. Jesus' salvation is free; if I believe, I receive it without further conditions. But discipleship is different. When Jesus said to the rich young man, "Go, sell everything you have... and follow me" (Mark 10:21) He was asking him to take a momentous step.

Either I believe that Jesus keeps His promises and my steps on the water will hold me up, or I doubt that all His words can be directly carried out. Will I really be repaid in this world for what I give away and leave behind, or will I be a fool in the end?

Today many Christians do the same thing as Jesus' listeners then: they make compromises. They are Jesus' followers, His fans, but not members of the inner circle of His disciples. They carry out certain of Jesus' instructions, they help here and there, but they retain the right to withdraw if what is asked becomes too extreme because they believe in "everything in moderation." What a pity!

Because Jesus promises unbelievable things to His disciples, i.e. to those who follow after Him. Things which everyone strives for: peace which no one can destroy (cf. John 14:27), lasting riches (cf. Mark 10:29-30), a light, easy burden. In other words: relief and rest. He instructs His disciples to keep His commands, that their lives may be filled with the joy of life (cf. John 15:11).

If these are all trustworthy promises, actual consequences of a lifestyle, how can a sensible person say no?

I repeat: the critical point is that we do not believe God. We are afraid of where we will end up if we let go of the tried and tested principles we have based our life upon. Our fear of loss and pain is greater than our trust in God.

A further hindrance is our pride. Whoever follows Jesus must submit to Him and obey Him. He must admit that he is no good to the core! He must be willing to be changed.

Jesus wants to lead each person back to his original purpose, which means the fulfillment of all his longings to be God's friend. A creature which is God's image and reflects His likeness. This sounds strange and a bit naïve, but it is true.

Jesus leads us back on this path for He, the Son of God, came to fetch us. But we must follow Him, or we will not reach this place where our dreams come true. Jesus shows us the path, but we must walk it ourselves. The path of discipleship is beautiful but not easy. We need the Holy Spirit who gives us joy, strengthens us and turns us around when we go astray. And we need people who have taken this path ahead of us, who encourage and help us understand Jesus' words. They can show us the path because they are a bit further ahead than we are and can look back. Like them, this book is a signpost which helps us walk the path Jesus shows us and continue to the end. It encourages us to set out on the adventure of discipleship.

My father has already traveled along a long path with Jesus and has learned much from Him. He tells about it in this book. The daily readings are not intellectual expositions of God's Word, but experiences with God. They are the testimony of a man who has followed God and learned to know Him. As his son, I know him in daily life and I can testify that he lives what he preaches in this book. He and my mother Regula can testify that Jesus keeps His promises and that it is absolutely worthwhile to follow Him.

The readings in this book are taken from a collection of sermons my father has given over the years. As a result some basic thoughts are taken up repeatedly and illuminated from different sides. This makes sense and is desirable – this repetition helps the reader grasp and assimilate the important topics he deals with.

I hope that as you read this book Jesus will encounter you and that you will be enthralled by the wonderful adventure of following Jesus.

You are included in the challenge to "come and follow me" (Matthew 4:19)!

Elija Rebiai
March 2008

Section 1

IN GOD'S IMAGE

He is the image of the invisible God, the firstborn over all creation. For by him all things were created: things in heaven and on earth, visible and invisible, whether thrones or powers or rulers or authorities; all things were created by him and for him. He is before all things, and in him all things hold together. And he is the head of the body, the church; he is the beginning and the firstborn from among the dead, so that in everything he might have the supremacy. For God was pleased to have all his fullness dwell in him, and through him to reconcile to himself all things, whether things on earth or things in heaven, by making peace through his blood, shed on the cross. Once you were alienated from God and were enemies in your minds because of your evil behavior. But now he has reconciled you by Christ's physical body through death to present you holy in his sight, without blemish and free from accusation...

(Colossians 1:15-22)

Day 1

WHO AM I?

One of the age-old questions which perturbs mankind is the question of our identity. Who is man, really? What is the essence of being a person? What is the meaning and goal of human existence? These questions are almost invariably linked to the question of God: Who or what is God? What is His true nature? If there is a God, where is He?

Since the beginning of time men have pondered these issues. Sundry philosophies and world views attempt to answer these questions. There are the totally materialistic concepts which claim that man is nothing more than a collection of atoms whose interaction as biological, chemical and physical forms of appearance determines man's behavior and existence. The opposite pole is the solely spiritual view, where man as a spirit must be liberated from all material enslavement in order to find his true destiny. Still other starting points contemplate man as the result of sociological and historical frameworks; of ethnic, cultural and familial factors. Each variant attempts to give some sort of answer to the question of who man is.

Why does this question about man drive us so relentlessly? I believe the answer is ultimately linked with a question which concerns us very personally, namely the question of our own identity. Who am I? Why am I? What am I all about? – Who is not searching deeply for himself!

Am I as others think of me? Am I that which I can achieve? Am I what my abilities make of me? Or am I simply a product of my personal history, and the coincidence which determined the framework of geography, culture, education and social position into which I was born?

I believe that the answer each person ultimately finds is a matter of faith. The Bible says in Hebrews, "By faith we understand..." (11:3). Some may say, "OK, but if I have no faith, how then can I understand?" I firmly claim that every person lives in a conscious or unconscious faith system. An atheist also has a faith. The fact that he says there is no God, without being able to prove this, shows that he proceeds on a hypothesis – in the hope that it will one day be proven. That makes the atheist a believer in something. We all have some kind of faith. The only question is which message we choose to believe. To whom do we open up? What do we consider true? From what available information will we ultimately draw our knowledge and conclusions in relation to ourselves and the world?

We all believe and the Bible says quite rightly, "By faith we understand..." If we now align ourselves with God's Word and put our faith in it, it will form and influence our view and our understanding of God, of man and of the world.

GETTING THE PICTURE

As early as Genesis 1 the Bible makes a very fundamental statement about man. There we read,

> So God created man in his own image, in the image of God he created him; male and female he created them.
>
> (1:27)

This means that mankind corresponds to God's image only as man and woman together. This statement is pivotal. If we hear God's Word and want to remain honest, it leads to difficulties. For if we look at man's behavior throughout history and if we assume that he is made in God's image, we get a very screwed-up picture of God. This makes us not only uneasy, but also fearful and without hope. The history of mankind is saturated with violence, war, destruction, greed and egoism. This relates not only to the present situation in the Near East, but such behavior is mankind's seal throughout history.

Thus, if we say that man is made in God's image, it is understandable that some human beings quickly turn away from such a God. An image of God derived through observation of men can cause fear and hopelessness. Man's unpredictability, his misuse and violation of his fellow human beings damages and even destroys the basis of trust. And trust is the essential precondition for developing a healthy life. Therefore God is often perceived as the punishing and judging God who is immutable in relation to mistakes and weaknesses. He is a God we fear because we always have the feeling He's looking over our shoulder – probably with a notebook in which He records each of our misdemeanors. Many people with a relationship to God still have this picture of Him.

During the course of history such a picture of God became an idol, with the result that the Christian Church persecuted and killed men in the name of God. Our picture of God always becomes an idol. And as we know, idols have hearts of stone because they are not alive. So what do we do with the biblical statement that God made man in His image?

And there is an additional problem in Exodus where God says, "You shall not make for yourself an image in the form of anything..." (20:4 TNIV). On the one hand it says, "Man is the image of God" and, on the other hand, "You shall not make for yourself an image of anything." How can we reconcile these two statements?

Here I claim that, if we are not to make an image of God, we should not make an image of man either, for he is God's image. Now all of us, if we are honest, are constantly busy making images on the basis of our experiences and knowledge because we cannot get our bearings or find our way without pictures. We speak of "getting the picture of something or someone." But God says we should not make images. When we make ourselves pictures of a person, we look at him primarily from the outside. When we define, classify, evaluate and judge people, we are always in danger of rendering them an injustice because we cannot see into their hearts. We judge from the outside, as it says in God's Word, "Man looks at the outward appearance, but the Lord looks at the heart" (1 Samuel 16:7c).

Over the centuries men have contrived a distorted picture of God. Just as this picture had noxious consequences, so can our picture of each other (with which we handcuff each other) destroy relationships. Why? Because we enter a relationship with our picture of a person rather than with the person himself.

Day 3

WHAT IS OUR PICTURE OF GOD?

If we want to understand who man is, we must listen to God and His Word. Since God made man in His own image, only He can give us the answer to our identity and destiny. If we want to find out something about the picture, "man," we must first study the original, "God." This makes it crucial to listen to what God says about Himself.

The question is, what do we know about God? What have we experienced with God? What sort of picture of God do we carry in our hearts? Who or what formed this picture? What does it arouse in us: trust – security – protection – peace? Or fear – anger – insecurity – exposure – and disappointment...? No one can say he has no picture of God. Each one of us carries some conception of God in himself. The question is only, what kind of conception?

If we want to find out something about God, the most reliable source is His own Word, the Bible. If we read and examine the prophets, the Torah (the first five books of the Bible) and the Psalms, we see first of all that the God of the Bible dwells in inaccessible light. For us He is unbearably perfect and holy. He is unbearably lovely and pure. God is so unapproachable for men that Moses, the prophet and man of God, had to say, "no one may see me and live" (Exodus 33:20b). It would be like the moth which flies too close to the light – he would inevitably be burned up.

We see further in God's Word that God is the unendingly merciful one: "The Lord, the Lord, the compassionate and gracious God, slow to anger, abounding in love and faithfulness" (Exodus 34:6b). God is a God who blesses to the thousandth generation and afflicts only to the third. He is unendingly patient. The New Testament says simply, "God is love. Whoever lives in love lives in God, and God in him" (1 John 4:16b).

Day 4

JESUS, THE IMAGE OF GOD

If we consider human realities – from egoism, introspection, mistrust, envy, lovelessness, pride and audacity to hatred and violence – we must admit that man has become a very damaged image of God. He can disclose little or only distorted information about the original template.

But thanks be to God that history does not end here, for the countenance of God became flesh! God revealed Himself to us in the man Jesus Christ. "He is the image of the invisible God" (Colossians 1:15) – this holy God whom we cannot reach because He dwells in inaccessible light. Man has long lost even an inkling of this God: God has become a stranger to us. This invisible, unendingly holy, perfect, lovely, pure and powerful God "became flesh and made his dwelling among us" (John 1:14). With this revelation He has profoundly surprised and even confused all of us.

God's self-revelation perturbed men. It often annoyed them greatly. Why? Because the disclosure took place in a way which made us feel very uncomfortable.

Who, being in very nature God, did not consider equality with God something to be grasped, but made himself nothing, taking the very nature of a servant, being made in human

likeness...he humbled himself and became obedient to death –
even death on a cross.

(Philippians 2:6-8)

This is how He had already been proclaimed by
the prophets.

> Rejoice greatly, O Daughter of Zion!
> Shout, Daughter of Jerusalem!
> See, your king comes to you, righteous and having salvation,
> gentle and riding on a donkey...

(Zechariah 9:9)

And Jesus said of Himself, "Come to me...and learn from me,
for I am gentle and humble in heart" (Matthew 11:28-29).

God reveals His countenance to us men in an unexpected
way. For thirty years He partook in the absolutely
unspectacular and ordinary daily lives of humans. This is
how close God comes to us – unbelievable!

Jesus said, "When a man...looks at me, he sees the one
who sent me" and "I and the Father are one" (John 12:44-45
and John 10:30). Only in Jesus do we see the pure and full
truth about God. He is the revelation of God in person. It is
very important that we write this indelibly into our hearts!
Apart from Jesus we can neither know God's countenance
nor draw near to Him. For God's true nature in grace and
truth, forgiveness and love became flesh in Jesus, the Son
of God.

The history of the past two thousand years has shown
that men have been driven not only by the question of who
man is and who God is, but also who Jesus is. This question
is still absolutely vital.

Day 5

GOD HAS DRAWN NEAR

In Jesus, God has come indescribably near us. Without hesitation, without prejudices. He was impressed neither with man's weakness, sin and failure nor with his strength, abilities and success. He sat down with the women and children who in His time were sidelined and considered second-class citizens. He cared about prostitutes and adulterers, restoring their dignity. He sat with lepers, outcasts and the poor. He dealt with usurers and tax collectors who were rightly despised, for they robbed their own people. He kept company with the soldiers who were the occupying power's lackeys and often misused their position of power. He socialized with the despised. He fraternized with those whom the people considered impure: godless foreigners, such as Samaritans and Romans. But also kept company with the self-righteous pious, the self-important intellectuals and the scholars. He accepted invitations to their parties and had fellowship with the doubters and godless, as well as with disciples and friends.

Jesus drew very, very close to all humanity. He did not withdraw even from those followers whom He knew would one day betray Him and abandon Him. He washed their feet in the face of the coming betrayal, in the face of the unimaginable loneliness and suffering ahead of Him.

In His humility, God came unbelievably close to men, holding onto hope for each individual's life. He kept the door open right to the end even for Judas when He greeted him as "my friend," thus inviting him to repent. That is God's nature. That is His countenance!

God made Himself highly vulnerable in choosing proximity to men. Closeness always includes the possibility of wounding because a heart of flesh is always vulnerable. Only a heart of stone cannot be wounded. God showed us His heart of flesh in Jesus. The price He paid for this vulnerability was humiliation, violation and torture on the cross. The proximity which God in Jesus showed to men demanded an unspeakably high price. God let men come very close to His heart – men with all their malice and mendacity, all their pride and self-righteousness, all their arrogance and over-estimation of themselves. He did not shrink from closeness to men. Why? Because He was not sent into the world to condemn it, but in order to save it (cf. John 3:17). Jesus came to save us and to bring us home.

BEING TRANSFORMED INTO HIS IMAGE

It is very difficult for us to grasp that this same God died for those who scorn, reject and hate Him. God loved us while we were still His enemies (cf. Romans 5:8). This is the character of God! He died for His enemies, took their guilt on Himself, suffered derision, mockery and rejection on the cross. He said, "Father, forgive them, for they do not know what they are doing" (Luke 23:34). That is the nature of God, who is love; the God who remains love to the end, who seeks and forgives the lost; the God who would have had every right to judge and destroy. But He waived this right in order to give men access to His presence.

Man was created in this image of God. Since the perfect image of God is revealed in Jesus, we read in Romans,

> For those God foreknew he also predestined to be conformed to the likeness of his Son, that he might be the firstborn among many brothers.
>
> (8:29)

The true calling and identity of man attains fulfillment through transformation into Jesus' likeness. Whenever our whole being, our heart and thoughts are saturated by the character of God's Son, we find our genuine humanness. We are created in this image of God. Jesus Himself is the sole source from which to nourish and understand our human identity.

I was touched by a news report about some missionaries who were murdered in April 2007 in Turkey. The attitude of the men's widows in their words to the press was very moving. The widow of a German missionary expressed it impressively and concisely. "We have only one message and one answer, namely the answer of our Lord on the cross, 'Father, forgive them, for they do not know what they do.'" The surprised journalist remarked that this woman's words had touched and moved the hearts of the Turkish people more strongly than decades of missionary work in the country. The power of forgiveness which he encountered in their response was strange to him. And it was that precisely which encapsulated the character of God under a spotlight.

Day 7

OUR TRUE CALLING

When we ponder God's image and absorb into our hearts and being His character and word, which became flesh in Jesus, we will be increasingly transformed into His likeness. And being transformed into Jesus' image is what our humanness, our discipleship and sonship are all about. God wants us to become people who are not afraid of closeness, people who can live in close proximity to all humanity, whatever their cultural, religious, historical or human backgrounds. If we know who God is and how eternally valuable we are to Him, we can also approach others without prejudice or fear. We will not allow ourselves to be impressed by their outward appearance.

God longs to retrieve us from darkness, guilt and estrangement from Himself. He wants to lead us into our true calling, as the likeness of His Son takes on form and reality within us. God wants us to have a heart of flesh, in His likeness; a heart permeated with forgiveness. A heart of flesh continually releases others from guilt and accusation and helps them make a new beginning. For as God's sons and daughters we are not called to judge, but to seek and save that which is lost.

Day 8

THERE IS HOPE FOR EACH ONE

With our whole being, we should transmit the good news that God has come very, very near to each and every one of us. God knows the very depths of our souls and has no illusions about us. He knows that we must be liberated from fear and from the enervating strain of having to protect ourselves continually. He knows that we have buttressed our hearts in self-defense, making it impossible for us to perceive our true inner condition or allow others to draw near us. He knows just how frozen our hard heart often is.

But that is just why Jesus came. He is Immanuel, God with us! If we seek His presence and His countenance daily, if we look at Him and ask Him to transform our hearts into His likeness, He will not disappoint us. There is nothing Jesus wants more than for the world to see His Father's countenance in us. He craves that mercy, veracity, humility, love, generosity and patience unfold in us. And there is nothing our heavenly Father wants more than our humbled and softened heart which holds up to Him the likeness of His beloved Son.

Jesus instructed, "learn from me, for I am gentle and humble in heart" (Matthew 11:29b). We will never understand our true human identity and calling except through Jesus, who was crucified and rose from the dead. He became for all of us a neighbor, friend and father, savior and protector. On the cross, the lowest point of His earthly life, He revealed the loving countenance of God. Don't give up hope. Jesus is the one of whom it was prophesied that "A bruised reed he will not break, and a smoldering wick he will not snuff out" (Isaiah 42:3 and Matthew 12:20). What an incredible message! What hope! This is the countenance of God in Jesus.

If we look at ourselves and deduce that in the face of our need and weakness there is little or no hope for us, if we are nearly crushed by our absolute inability to change, if we suffer because of our deep-seated pride, our inferiority complex, our morbid mistrust and fear of being cut short – then we should hold fast to the fact that Jesus does not break the bruised reed or snuff out a smoldering wick (until He has completed His will in us). This is where faith begins – when we come to Him and cling to Him with the desperation of a drowning person. If God really is God, then there is hope for each one of us. If we reach out to Him with our whole heart, He will transform us into His likeness step by step. Then others will see God in us, will experience Him and draw hope. In this way, many will break through to life, to freedom and to God's joy.

Section 2

~~

YOUR KING COMES TO YOU

Rejoice greatly, Daughter Zion!
Shout, Daughter Jerusalem!
See, your king comes to you,
righteous and having salvation,
lowly and riding on a donkey,
on a colt, the foal of a donkey.
I will take away the chariots from Ephraim
and the warhorses from Jerusalem,
and the battlebow will be broken.
He will proclaim peace to the nations.
His rule will extend from sea to sea and from
the River to the ends of the earth.

(Zechariah 9:9-10 TNIV)

Day 9

JESUS COMES IN AN UNEXPECTED WAY

The mystery of Christmas, the birth of Jesus, is that God Himself enters His own creation. We hear this, nod and take it for granted because we have already heard it so often. But if we are honest, it doesn't really move us.

Perhaps the reason for this is that we don't really understand what God's incarnation means for the world. In addition, the story of the Messiah's coming into this world is told in a way which is difficult for us to comprehend. It was difficult for the Jewish people both then and now, as well as for all the other peoples, even though the prophet Zechariah calls to Jerusalem, Zion, and the Jewish people, "Rejoice greatly!" Why? "Your king is coming to you." At first we can understand this, for here we are told that this king is "righteous and a helper" or in some translations "righteous and victorious." This is something which we can all grasp, for somewhere and somehow we are all searching for help. Therefore if we are seeking a king, we seek one who is victorious and a helper. Up to here we all say "amen," happy about the help we are finally receiving.

But then the prophet continues his description. This king is "poor – or lowly – and riding on a donkey." Instead of "poor" some translations read "humble." It is difficult for us to think of these traits in connection with a victorious king from whom we expect help. For we know the principle that the world belongs to the strong and the victorious, to those who can get their own way, the successful, the self-assured, those who know who they are and what they can do, who are aware of their rights and can insist on them. Therefore, when speaking about John the Baptist, Jesus makes the strange comment, "the kingdom of heaven has been subjected to violence, and violent people have been raiding it" (Matthew 11:12 TNIV).

Day 10

THE RIGHT OF THE STRONG

This world's reality is that by means of force and violence, or by means of their abilities, people can manipulate, suppress and subject others – whether physically, emotionally or intellectually – thus compelling them to submit to their will. This is force. Force makes people subservient, and there's nothing they can do about it.

In God's kingdom, also, people often attempt to use power through violence, pressure or intimidation. This misuse of power utilizes not only legalism and narrow-mindedness, but also a so-called tolerance, as well as a humanistic way of thinking. It can behave very aggressively toward all those who think differently.

No one in this world wants to be on the side of the failures, the inarticulate, the insecure. Everyone wants to be on the side of the eloquent, who are quite aware of their identity, what they have to offer and what they are worth. So we are now offered thousands of therapy courses and self-expression groups where the goal is to find ourselves, where we can finally realize ourselves in the way which is good for us and which leads to the fulfillment of our goals, wishes and dreams. The world is screaming for help. And if it searches for a helper or a king, then one who surpasses them in everything, one who says, "I'm stronger, more successful and more capable than all of you. And I'll show you the way to success."

This world is hard. Only those who fend for themselves survive. Therefore we learn from an early age how to use our elbows in order to get ahead.

Day 11

SUCCESS AND POVERTY

And now a humble, poor king enters a world which is seeking success and power. But who wants to be subject to a poor king? Such a king cannot buy or accumulate anything in this world. As the proverb says, money rules the world! A humble person will not be respected, but will be ridiculed by the powerful and violent. He doesn't play by the world's rules, so what can he possibly hope to achieve? For a humble person will surely not elbow his way through. He will not manipulate or misuse others for his own aims, nor will he make others compliant because that would be incompatible with humility. Only self-confident people who focus solely on themselves and their goals use those kinds of methods.

With justified shock the person who has grown up with the laws of this world asks: Why did God choose this path? He, to whom all ways are open, chose the most irrational one. A path which surely leads to downfall and death. A lamb in the midst of wolves! God sends a humble one, a poor one into this world, although He knows that the Jewish people and the nations are watching for something totally different.

This helper-king not only comes poor, powerless and without any resources, He even comes to absolutely unspectacular, ordinary, simple people – people who are not prominent in any way, who would normally be simply overlooked. I can imagine that Joseph and Mary were such inconspicuous people who deferred to others. The Scriptures say little about them. It is not written that they had a special place in their village. The only thing said of Mary is that she pondered in her heart everything she heard.

Day 12

What was there about Joseph and Mary that God entrusted His Son to them?

God entrusts His Son to inconspicuous people. We would understand better if God's Son, this central figure in human history, had come into the world via an aristocratic family or influential people. As a strategist God is difficult to understand in our eyes. He let His Son come into this world in a remote stable, instead of in Jerusalem's high-priestly family; or at least among people who could have immediately made Him known. The only people who noticed Him there were a few shepherds. This is not our way of thinking.

I asked myself what there was about Joseph and Mary that made it possible for God to entrust Himself to them? Then I realized that there is a great difference between God giving people His gifts and God entrusting Himself to them. Many people have gifts from God. For example, the high priest Caiaphas had the gift of prophecy. It is written that Caiaphas prophesied, because he was high priest at that time, that one had to suffer for all (cf. John 11:49-51). God can bestow gifts on people without entrusting Himself to them. I am always touched by John 2:24,

But Jesus would not entrust himself to them, for he knew all men.

Joseph and Mary were obviously people to whom God entrusted Himself. They were open for something which God deemed essential and they had no hidden agenda. We see this in Mary. After the angel had spoken to her, she did not open a discussion with Him. Even though she asked, "How shall this be...?" (Luke 1:34) she was satisfied with the angel's reply, "God will do it." She didn't say, "Do you know what this will mean for me? I have to think it over carefully. I can't just say yes because I might be labeled a prostitute. I agree on the condition that you explain it to the others so they won't have the wrong impression of me. I will agree if you see to it that I don't lose face."

These days when God asks something of us, whether directly or through another person, we say, "I have to pray about it" or, "I have to think it over." This is how seriously we take ourselves – our decisions, our possibilities, what we can or cannot cope with. We walk around with our hand on our pulse and when challenged we ask, "Can I manage? Is it good for me? Where will it lead? What will it bring me? What damage could it cause me?"

Day 13

GOD LOVES THE SIMPLE IN HEART

Mary exhibits none of these concerns. She even says, "I am the Lord's servant. May it be unto me as you have said" (Luke 1:38). This is simplicity! If God says something, we don't have to worry about how He will do it. Mary understood that God is God and what He plans, He will also do.

Mary must have been a woman with an unpretentious disposition, a woman who in the truest sense was simple before God. She did not consider her honor or her own goals important. She took the risk that Joseph, her betrothed, the essence of her future and her dreams, would misunderstand and abandon her. Mary took God more seriously than everything else, more than even her own hopes and goals.

God seeks out such people to entrust Himself to – not His gifts, but Himself. God gives His gifts to many people. But even when He does so and these people lead others to faith through their gifts, or can build great things, this still says nothing about God's intimate relationship with them.

In Isaiah 57:15 we read,

[T]his is what the high and lofty One says –
he who lives for ever, whose name is holy:
"I live in a high and holy place,
but also with him who is contrite and lowly in spirit."

A contrite, broken spirit is a spirit that absolutely no longer counts on itself. A broken spirit has profoundly understood that God alone is important, not one's own potential, goals and dreams. To such people, God says, I will entrust Myself personally.

Day 14

THE SOURCE OF SIN

Why did God send His Son? Why did He Himself come to this world in His Son? We quickly answer, "In order to save us and take us out of darkness." But what has destroyed our lives? What has driven us into death and brought our death sentence upon the whole creation? Was it not the reality of pride, presumption and arrogance?

The prophets Isaiah and Ezekiel use the kings of Tyre and Babylon to describe the fall of Lucifer, the angel of light (cf. Isaiah 14:3-19 and Ezekiel 28:1-19). Lucifer, who was created in perfect beauty, glory and power, left the place allotted to him and wanted to be God. The fullness of power and glory had made his heart proud, so that he forgot that everything he was and had was a gift from the creator and he himself was still His creature. In spite of all his wisdom and his great power, he had obviously not understood that the unbridgeable chasm between God the creator and His creatures can never be overcome with might, knowledge and force, but only through love and dedication. The devil rose up against God, bringing on himself and all who followed him darkness, destruction and death.

Since then, pride, presumption and arrogance have been the source of sin. Pride is the essence of sin and leads ultimately to the death of man and of creation. Since the Fall every person's life has been founded on pride. Everything which grows in this soil – our definition of power, glory and the fulfillment of everything we associate with life – is poisoned.

Jesus' life was a complete antithesis to our ideas and our pride. He had to tear down everything man had built up since the Fall. Jesus can begin with a person only from the very bottom, where all presumption, all pride and arrogance are judged under the cross and the person confesses, "God, have mercy on me, a sinner!" (Luke 18:13). Whoever is unwilling to set out from this point has no way to enter the kingdom of God.

Day 15

HUMILITY IS GOD'S REMEDY

Humility is God's remedy. This characteristic, this heavenly elixir, roots out and totally destroys pride. Jesus' being is absolutely foreign to this world. We often have the impression that humility is something lovely, a good Christian virtue. Of course we know that humility is not simply a matter of lowering our eyes when someone looks at us, or shyly retreating to the back row. Nor does it mean making ourselves worse than we are, playing down our gifts and emphasizing our weak points a bit more. Humility is the attitude of Jesus which expresses that God alone is important, that He alone is life and His word is absolutely trustworthy. Humility is the remedy for the proud person, the protective covering for our heart in this world. There is only one thing the devil cannot bear: the fragrance of genuine humility. Without God, man is a nothing, says the Bible – not simply "not so good," but simply clay, earth.

Jesus could come into the world only in a place men normally avoid – in a stable, in poverty and cold, on the fringe of society. Humility had to be visible from the beginning, at Jesus' birth. The wonderful thing is that this place is accessible for every person. The shepherd and the king can enter this stable. Not everyone is allowed into a palace. But God says, "It is really possible for every person to come to Me and everyone who comes should know that in a stable all are equal."

Day 16

GOD DWELLS WITH SIMPLE PEOPLE

Do you realize where God likes to be? Right in the place we try to avoid at all cost! Who wants to be unimportant? Who wants to belong to the poor and the simple? Who wants to live in the most remote place, where no one notices him, where there is a poor communications system, not even Internet? A place where we can't express ourselves? "But that's exactly where I am," says God. What wonderful news!

"Who am I anyway?" we often think, and then exaggerate a bit. "I'm useless to God because I'm so weak and untalented, because I was so emotionally wounded during my childhood, because of my upbringing, and so on."

All this hinders God from using us. But if we're really convinced that we're unimportant and have nothing to bring – and if this is not just another way to make ourselves important and to use others' pity for our own life energy – if we truly believe we are poor und unimportant, then the good news of Christmas is for us, the news that these are exactly the kind of people Jesus wants to dwell with. He is happy about people who say with their whole hearts, "Lord, I am Your servant. Come to me. You can do anything You want in my life." And then He might well take us down a very unspectacular route.

I sometimes imagine what Mary must have been thinking during those thirty years before Jesus' public ministry. She knew that He was the Messiah. She saw Him washing up, sweeping wood chips, fetching water… and kept thinking: "He's already twenty, already twenty-five, and still nothing is happening. Nothing is changing in the world. And yet He is the one who is to save the whole world!" Can you imagine what was going on in her heart?

Day 17

DISCIPLESHIP IS NOT SHOW BUSINESS

If God enters our lives, He often takes us on a totally unspectacular path. He lets fruit ripen in our hearts until it is really tasty. We would prefer to see our tree full of fruit on the next day, in order to prove that God has really come to us. Or at least that there would be some special aura around us for people to recognize how special we are. This does not express the attitude, "Lord, I am Your servant. Your will be done in me," but rather, "I'd like something in advance." This hurts God because we are really saying, "You aren't enough for me. I would like to profit outwardly as well. I want others to notice that I'm taking a spiritual path and that my life is fruitful."

Can we picture how long people who knew Mary waited, all the while surmising, "If it's true that an angel came to her and her son is really the Messiah, then we should see something!" But for thirty years nothing happened. God expects this of us.

But this period is not in vain because He is working in our hearts and wants to become very familiar to us. God knows that the more familiar He is to us, the less vulnerable we are when we take His kingdom out into the world. If we are convinced that we have nothing to give and really are poor, weak and insignificant, that we are like a stable – musty, dusty and smelly and like the animals it houses as stubborn as a mule and as hard-necked as an ox, – then we can know that this is exactly where God likes to come and begin building His kingdom. We hinder God with our pride and our selfishness; we hinder Him when we are overly concerned about our weaknesses, our wounds and our past, about things in our lives which we find so terrible that God should please take a good look at them...

It is up to us whether God can entrust Himself to us. Are we interested in His gifts only in order to build something in His name, or something which bears our own name as well? God wants to give out His gifts because He needs many people who build things in His name and with His gifts. But that doesn't automatically mean that these people are also His confidantes. Let's not forget this. Now we can understand the word,

"So the last will be first, and the first will be last."

(Matthew 20:16)

In other words, "Be watchful. The first, who build many things with many gifts, could find themselves among the last. And this world's inconspicuous people, who don't show so much outwardly, could turn out to be the first." Why? Because God likes to entrust Himself to inconspicuous people who live in intimate fellowship with Him, even if – as with Mary – this is not outwardly visible.

Section 3

RESURRECTION – HEAVEN LAUGHS

If Christ has not been raised, our preaching is useless and so is your faith. More than that, we are then found to be false witnesses about God, for we have testified about God that he raised Christ from the dead. But he did not raise him if in fact the dead are not raised. For if the dead are not raised, then Christ has not been raised either. And if Christ has not been raised, your faith is futile; you are still in your sins. Then those also who have fallen asleep in Christ are lost. If only for this life we have hope in Christ, we are to be pitied more than all men. But Christ has indeed been raised from the dead, the firstfruits of those who have fallen asleep.

(1 Corinthians 15:14-20)

Day 18

WHY IS THE RESURRECTION NECESSARY?

For Paul, the resurrection is the central event in Jesus' life, together with the crucifixion. The resurrection is the ultimate confirmation of what happened on the cross. Modern man may find it difficult to grasp why the resurrection had such radical meaning for Paul – but not the Jews of that time. They believed that it became clear only at the end of a person's life whether God approved of him and confirmed his calling – whether the things he had said and done were really from God.

In Psalm 22:8 the psalmist foretold the people's opinion of the suffering servant of God, the Messiah,

"He trusts in the Lord; let the Lord rescue him.
Let him deliver him, since he delights in him."

Here we see that the people expected God not to allow His servant and messiah to perish. If God was pleased with him, if God really stood by him when he acted in God's name, then God should intervene and save him. After all, it says in Psalm 37:18:

The days of the blameless are known to the Lord,
and their inheritance will endure for ever.

If God did not intervene, that proves that the message was meaningless.

Remember the advice the Jewish scholar Rabbi Gamaliel gave the Jewish court which was judging the apostles,

> "Leave these men alone! Let them go! For if their purpose or activity is of human origin, it will fail. But if it is from God, you will not be able to stop these men; you will only find yourselves fighting against God."
>
> (Acts 5:38-39)

The meaning of resurrection is absolutely central in connection with the cross. God set His signature on Jesus' message through the resurrection – thus confirming not only the message, but the very person of Jesus.

Day 19

GOD ENDORSES JESUS' DEATH

In John 11:25-26 Jesus says,

> "I am the resurrection and the life. He who believes in me will
> live, even though he dies; and whoever lives and believes in me
> will never die."

When Jesus links the resurrection, the victory over death
and the hope of eternal life to His own person, He is
speaking ultimately about the consummation of His life
mission. This no longer concerns simply His teaching, but
it is about Him as a person. So we can understand the Jews'
fear. It was not only that the disciples could have stolen the
corpse: the Jews deeply feared that God could actually put
His signature on the life of this enigmatic person. If God
wakened Jesus from the dead, something with unforeseeable
consequences could be set in motion. This fear is expressed
in Matthew 27:64,

> "So give the order for the tomb to be made secure until the
> third day. Otherwise, his disciples may come and steal the body
> and tell the people that he has been raised from the dead. This
> last deception would be worse than the first."

After the resurrection the leading Jews could think of no way to help themselves except by bribing the sentries to deny resurrection, as we read in Matthew 28:12-13,

> When the chief priests had met with the elders and devised a plan, they gave the soldiers a large sum of money, telling them, "You are to say, 'His disciples came during the night and stole him away while we were asleep.'"

The miracle of the resurrection is not just something God did with Jesus. This resurrection is not the same as when other people are raised from the dead, as still happens among His disciples. Jesus' resurrection set God's signature on the prophecy in Isaiah 53,

> Surely he took up our infirmities and carried our sorrows,
> yet we considered him stricken by God,
> smitten by him, and afflicted.
> But he was pierced for our transgressions,
> he was crushed for our iniquities;
> the punishment that brought us peace was upon him,
> and by his wounds we are healed...
> though the Lord makes his life a guilt offering,
> he will see his offspring and prolong his days,
> and the will of the Lord will prosper in his hand...
> by his knowledge my righteous servant will justify many,
> and he will bear their iniquities.
>
> (vv. 4-5, 10-11)

Jesus refers to this prophecy when He says of Himself, "the Son of Man did not come to be served, but to serve, and to give his life as a ransom for many" (Matthew 20:28).

Day 20

THE MEANING OF THE CROSS

The cross was not only a gruesome Roman method of execution; to the Jews the cross, or the tree, was also a place without God, a cursed place, as we read in Deuteronomy 21:23, "anyone who is hung on a tree is under God's curse." According to Jewish thought it was not only unreasonable, but also heresy that the Messiah himself, the expected savior of Israel, the second David, should end on the cross as a sign of sin's curse and God's absence.

The cross is likewise an insult to so-called common sense. The cross is an unbearable offence for everyone who believes that by means of his intellect and good will man can ultimately overcome evil and bring forth good. It is a clamorous testimony to the fact that man cannot bear what is truly good and pure in his midst. He destroys it and thus confirms God's word about mankind in Romans 3:10-12,

> There is no-one righteous, not even one; there is no-one who understands; no-one who seeks God. All have turned away, they have together become worthless; there is no-one who does good, not even one.

Because God knows man's situation, He sent the only One who Himself knew nothing of the sin of pride, egoism, falsehood and arrogance; He called this One to take the death-bringing reality of man's guilt on Himself – this guilt which stood between God and man – and carry it away to the cursed tree. We read in 2 Corinthians 5:21,

> God made him who had no sin to be sin for us, so that in him we might become the righteousness of God.

Jews and non-Jews alike are incurably guilty before God. There is no one who is righteous, not even one! So we can understand why Jesus said that He did not come to call the righteous, but the sinners. There are no righteous! There are only those who admit that they are deathly ill in soul and spirit and need help, or those who refuse to accept their condition and ultimately perish in their pride.

Day 21

THERE IS NONE WHO IS RIGHTEOUS

If God's Passover Lamb had not been slaughtered for us, the angel of judgment, the death angel, would not pass by any of us! The prophet Isaiah said,

> We all, like sheep, have gone astray,
> each of us has turned to his own way;
> and the Lord has laid on him the iniquity of us all.
>
> (Isaiah 53:6)

From that time on the decision regarding salvation and damnation, life and death, has depended solely on the One on whom God laid the guilt of all. Since the event on the cursed tree, no one can get around this One, neither Jew nor non-Jew, even though this message is a massive stumbling block for Jews and great foolishness to non-Jews, according to Paul (see 1 Corinthians 1:22-23). Forgiveness of guilt and salvation from death and destruction come only through the blood of God's Passover Lamb, not through man's good deeds or religious efforts.

At the cross the idea of a good and reasonable mankind is exposed as a lie. Man's pride is shaken to the core. God's Lamb who bore our guilt on the cursed tree, perishing miserably because of it, becomes the sole gate which leads to life and freedom. But we can pass through this narrow, low gate only by bending over. None can go through without his pride being broken. But whoever refuses to bend over and place his pride under the judgment which for his sake was carried out on Jesus will find himself rebelling when confronted with God's judgment on his life. Rejection, mockery, contempt and hatred – harbingers of darkness, death and damnation – will reach for his heart and draw him ever deeper into estrangement and enmity with the God of the Bible.

Without the resurrection as God's signature on Jesus' message, it would have been nothing more than a philosophy or a mystic's view which would no more have changed people's hearts than any other philosophy or religion. Nothing in the world would have been moved.

Day 22

NO ONE COMES TO THE FATHER BUT THROUGH ME

The resurrection is God's clear message that there is no other access to Him than through His Son's sacrifice. It confirms Jesus' two statements in John's Gospel:

> "I am the way and the truth and the life. No-one comes to the Father except through me."
>
> (John 14:6)

> "For God did not send his Son into the world to condemn the world, but to save the world through him. Whoever believes in him is not condemned, but whoever does not believe stands condemned already because he has not believed in the name of God's one and only Son."
>
> (John 3:17-18)

There is no other path except the confession, "Lord, I can do nothing. Be merciful to me, a poor sinner, because I really deserve death." The cross is the place where God calls each one of us to experience grace, salvation and help in judgment. There is no detour, no shortcut. No one can come directly to the God of love. Access to the God of love is only through the truth at the cross. God is love and His love became visible when His heart let His Son go through the agony of judgment and death for you and me. There was no other way to destroy pride and arrogance or to save us from eternal darkness and separation from God. No one loves us more! No one can understand why God did this for us. Nor can love be understood. It can be experienced only by loving in return.

There is another aspect of God's character which is difficult for us to grasp: unless we accept Jesus' sacrifice, there is only judgment without mercy. In Hebrews 10:31 we read,

> It is a dreadful thing to fall into the hands of the living God.

God is love, but we can experience this love only in connection with the cross. If we do not comprehend that judgment is an absolute reality over this world and our life, we will never understand the meaning of the resurrection. God calls the world and each one of us to the cross.

God can spare no one the disgrace of the cross; each one of us will have to experience it. It is the door to life and to grace. When we go to the cross the world will see us. People will watch and react. We ourselves will experience the offence which the cross means for the world. If we stand under the cross and identify ourselves with it, we will forcefully encounter the indignation of those who believe in man, whether they are religious, secular or atheistic, whether materialistic or social, whatever their background.

Day 23

RESURRECTION IS A NEW CREATION

But when we really come to the cross we will realize what resurrection is. It is not only the breakthrough of God's kingdom into this world and our life. Resurrection is a new creation! Jesus' resurrection means nothing less than the fact that from now on there is a new heaven and a new earth! Resurrection means that mankind now has a new family tree which was founded by the Son! Man becomes a member of God's family! A new family of God began in and with Jesus.

Resurrection means that God went much further than in the first creation. In the first creation He created the world and man, then gave him this world to live in, and entered into a relationship with him. But God in His essence was not yet part of man's existence. Only in Jesus has He become part of us. Therefore, whoever identifies himself with Jesus and His death on the cross also participates in Jesus' resurrection. He is thus born into God's kingdom.

Our natural history with all its pernicious influence of blood relationship, with its familial and cultural compulsions, our imprisonment in the images others make of us and the words they express over us – all this reaches its final end at the cross, as John said,

Yet to all who received him, to those who believed in his name, he gave the right to become children of God – children born not of natural descent, nor of human decision or a husband's will, but born of God.

(John 1:12-13)

For our small heart – and even more for our intellect – it is far from easy to understand or believe this amazing message. Through Jesus' resurrection we are no longer merely creatures within this creation, but a new creation!

Therefore, if anyone is in Christ, he is a new creation; the old has gone, the new has come!

(2 Corinthians 5:17)

The Holy Spirit has given birth to us as sons and daughters of God, in His family. In Romans 8:16-17 we read,

The Spirit himself testifies with our spirit that we are God's children. Now if we are children, then we are heirs – heirs of God and co-heirs with Christ...

But resurrection also means that judgment is abolished once and for all.

Therefore, there is now no condemnation for those who are in Christ Jesus...

(Romans 8:1)

Day 24

No more fear

Jesus' resurrection confirms that His substitutionary death on the cross overcame once and for all the powers of darkness and death which separated man from God and thus from life; it confirms that everyone who belongs to Him is no longer at their mercy. Those who belong to Him have no more reason to fear because fear means we do not know God; it means we are at the mercy of the powers which destroy life. This is more than just a matter of our bodies – these are powers which can destroy us in all eternity.

Jesus calls to us, "In this world you will have trouble [some German translations say 'fear']. But take heart! I have overcome the world" (John 16:33). Whoever through Jesus entrusts himself to God's love, and holds fast to it, will know that "There is no fear in love" (1 John 4:18). From now on we have a Father who loves us with the same love He has for His only Son Jesus! This Father calls to us,

> "For I know the plans I have for you," declares the Lord, "plans to prosper you and not to harm you, plans to give you hope and a future."
>
> (Jeremiah 29:11)

Resurrection means that my hope is a living hope because it is established in the living God. My future can be destroyed neither by economic catastrophes nor atomic bombs. My future cannot be destroyed by anything because God guarantees it and says to me, through Paul,

> Rejoice in the Lord always. I will say it again: Rejoice!...Do not be anxious about anything, but in everything, by prayer and petition, with thanksgiving, present your requests to God. And the peace of God, which transcends all understanding, will guard your hearts and your minds in Christ Jesus.
>
> (Philippians 4:4, 6-7)

See also 1 Peter 5:7,

> Cast all your anxiety on him because he cares for you.

Through Jesus' resurrection we were not only born into God's kingdom: His kingdom was also born in our heart like a mustard seed. It grows and penetrates our life with His kingdom character which is peace, joy, freedom from worry, confidence, calmness, trust, forgiveness, goodness, love... In Jesus we are called to life, to joy and to peace! The only thing still exposed to this world, to which death still has access, is my body – but even that is ultimately in God's hands. My body belongs to a dying and transient world. Therefore Jesus says, "do not be afraid of those who kill the body and after that can do no more" (Luke 12:4).

Day 25

A NEW REALITY

Through the resurrection our lives have entered a new reality which is independent of our external circumstances. Because our lives are in our heavenly Father's hands, nothing can now destroy our hope and our peace – not even bereavement, illness, unemployment or accident. God promises that everything we encounter must serve to our best. Only on the basis of the resurrection can we understand that although we are still part of this world, our whole being belongs to another kingdom. Jesus did not remove us from this world because through us He wants to demonstrate the reality of His resurrection in this world.

As God's children we live in the resurrection reality. It is not that some day we will enter God's kingdom; we belong to it already because Jesus, who is the light living in us, called us to be a light in the darkness of this world. He says to us, "You are the light of the world" (Matthew 5:14). The people around us – whom God loves so much that He gave His heart to save them – should, in the midst of their need, hopelessness, bitterness, loneliness and fear, see our eyes lit up with God's countenance. In us they should encounter God's peace, joy, hope, forgiveness, goodness and care. Then they will find the way to the cross, the way to the Father's heart, the way back home.

We have every reason to testify to this peace and this hope, for we have been liberated to a life with an inconceivable future. This is a future which surpasses every concept of happiness, joy and beauty, as Paul says in 1 Corinthians 2:9,

> "No eye has seen, no ear has heard, no mind has conceived what God has prepared for those who love him…"

And in Romans 8:18,

> I consider that our present sufferings are not worth comparing with the glory that will be revealed in us.

Our goal is perfection, joy and peace; a new heaven and a new earth which will be immersed in light, peace, joy and beauty! This is not just an illusion or cheap comfort, but reality – as real as the reality that God is the creator of heaven and earth, the reality that He raised Jesus from the dead! May God increasingly permeate those of us who belong to Jesus with an awareness of the resurrection; with the awareness that we have an indestructible future because Jesus lives in us.

Until we reach perfection – when God calls us home to Himself or Jesus returns – our lives remain a daily struggle against everything which distracts us from our Father and His growing and coming kingdom in us.

Day 26

THE RESURRECTION LETS US OVERCOME

Troubles and problems will never be absent as we follow Jesus on the path home, for small is the gate and narrow the road which lead to life. Sometimes we suffer from ourselves, i.e. from our inability to love, trust or be truthful. The more we allow God's kingdom to spread in our hearts, the more this suffering will decrease. But there is also suffering for the sake of God's kingdom because darkness persecutes light with all the means at its disposal. Paul wrote of this in 2 Corinthians 6:4-10,

> Rather, as servants of God we commend ourselves in every way: in great endurance; in troubles, hardships and distresses; in beatings, imprisonments and riots...through glory and dishonor, bad report and good report; genuine, yet regarded as impostors; known, yet regarded as unknown;...sorrowful, yet always rejoicing; poor, yet making many rich; having nothing, and yet possessing everything!

In everything we are more than conquerors through Him who loved us – Jesus, the Risen One! We think about the resurrection not only during the Easter season, when it is a tradition. No, for us it is absolutely necessary to reflect on Jesus' resurrection daily because the resurrection's reality is the mightiest force in all of creation. It is the only thing which can change our lives and continue to preserve them until the day of His return.

In the resurrection, eternity has broken into our hearts. Our future is clarified and certain. In spite of all the pressures and tensions which may accompany us, we do not have to cheat our way through life with some sort of anesthetic. People sedate themselves when they have no hope and no future, when they do not know why they have been saved and thus cannot face the end confrontation with the result of sin. "For the wages of sin is death" (Romans 6:23). But when we have grasped the power of the resurrection and have begun to live in it, we need fear neither death nor the devil!

Day 27

THE FEAST OF LAUGHTER

We want to witness to the incomparably joyful message that death and the devil have been conquered. Now darkness can be overcome in the life of every person who comes to Jesus! We want to witness to the resurrection with our whole life and with a joyful heart. We have every reason to do so! Let us join in God's laughter. In the early days of church history, Easter was also known as the feast of laughter, referring to Psalm 2:4,

> The One enthroned in heaven laughs; the Lord scoffs at them.

What does He scoff at? At all the powers who say they will destroy God's creation, those who thought they had thwarted God's plans when His Messiah perished miserably on the cross. The powers of evil knew God only as holy, just and merciless regarding sin. Therefore they thought that the Messiah had broken down under the burden of sin. They did not know God as love and did not know that love can take unimaginable paths.

I can imagine that the inhabitants of heaven were also initially shocked by the darkness of the cross, but then broke out in hearty laughter with God when Jesus rose from the grave on the third day. Only then did both angels and demons alike realize that God's judgment is not the end, but the beginning. Through death and judgment God's love created a door to life, to the Father's house. In the deepest darkness the brightest light shone. Once and for all it became clear to every power that in His Messiah Jesus God's hand reached down into the deepest depths of darkness and sin and death; He did this to save everyone who will ever call on the name of the Lord. Where the devil thought he had won, he suffered this crushing defeat. The final defeat of evil filled heaven with laughter. That is why the resurrection is a daily feast of laughter for us!

Day 28

IF GOD IS FOR US, WHO CAN BE AGAINST US?

The devil wants to convince us that God cannot reach His goal with us because we are such failures – people like us with such a ruined past, unstable character, impossible circumstances haven't a chance. When the devil besets us with hopelessness and resignation we can just take a big step back and, looking at the Resurrected One, laugh and say: You don't know God's heart! If you knew who God is and what He has done and is still doing for me, you would slink off! I fear neither you nor the reality of my own life, for there is nothing in this creation which cannot be changed and overcome through Jesus' resurrection power! How could God – after doing the inconceivable for me – now desert me? Don't you know that He has given me everything for my life to thrive?

> What, then, shall we say in response to this [when we are tempted]? If God is for us, who can be against us? He who did not spare his own Son, but gave him up for us all – how will he not also, along with him, graciously give us all things?
>
> (Romans 8:31-32)

This is cause for joy! As long as we cling to Jesus we can erase hopelessness, resignation, fear and loneliness from our vocabulary without becoming utopian! Every day His forgiveness, His hope, His goodness and His power are freshly available to change our lives so they are filled with peace and joy. Through the Messiah Jesus, the prophet Jeremiah calls to us, "his compassions never fail. They are new every morning; great is your faithfulness" (Lamentations 3:22b-23).

Every morning when we awake and place ourselves under the rule of Jesus, the Son of God, we can joyfully remind ourselves: God's thoughts for us today are thoughts of peace, salvation and joy. He has given us a glorious, indestructible future! Let us proclaim this joyful message to all people, for that is the desire of God's heart.

Section 4

THE DESERT

Then Jesus was led by the Spirit into the desert to
be tempted by the devil. After fasting forty days
and forty nights, he was hungry. The tempter
came to him...

(Matthew 4:1-3)

"For where your treasure is,
there your heart will be also."

(Matthew 6:21)

"They overcame him by the blood of the Lamb
and by the word of their testimony; they did not
love their lives so much as to shrink from death."

(Revelation 12:11)

Day 29

WHY DO WE FOLLOW JESUS?

What do these three texts have in common? A lot, I believe, for our ongoing theme as Jesus' disciples is loving Him and following Him. On this path of discipleship we are promised the fullness of life, as we read in John 10:10b, "I have come that they may have life, and have it to the full." But if we are honest, reality often looks quite different. We certainly do not always experience this fullness. Why do so many Christians lack peace, joy, comfort and calm?

In order to find some answers we must first ask ourselves why we became Christians in the first place. It is seldom love for Jesus which leads a person to this decision. I believe that it is usually based on an instinct for self-preservation, i.e. on selfish motives. Some became Christians from fear of hell, which is a legitimate reason, because without salvation through Jesus' cross we would surely be lost. But this has everything to do with ourselves and little to do with God. Others became Christians because they hoped for Jesus' help and support in their marriage; still others because they could not cope with life and thus accepted the offer to become whole, to receive a helping hand to get out of their troubles.

These are all legitimate motives, for Jesus Himself calls to us,

> "Come to me, all you who are weary and burdened, and I will give you rest [help you]. Take my yoke upon you and learn from me, for I am gentle and humble in heart, and you will find rest for your souls. For my yoke is easy and my burden is light."
>
> (Matthew 11:28-30)

Day 30

SELFISH MOTIVES

So we often come to God in order to receive something. We want to be helped and become whole. Our eyes are fixed firmly on ourselves and our motives are selfish. It is not just that our first steps toward Jesus are usually selfish. Later we can even serve Him or go to the mission field from egotistic motives. God knows this very well! He knows our hearts to the core and thus has no illusions. But God's greatness becomes visible precisely when He is involved with us in spite of our egoism. He accepts us as we are.

But God does not merely want to satisfy our acute hunger or only lead us into life's fullness. He wants to lead us close to His heart, for we can find rest nowhere else. So He does not leave us as we are. He begins familiarizing us with the principles of His kingdom. According to these principles, we don't find life by grabbing for it, but by being willing to lose it by letting ourselves fall into God's hands (see Matthew 10:39). If we don't realize this we will never really understand what it is to be Jesus' disciple.

God is so great that He responds with peace and joy to our first selfish steps. Everyone who has truly encountered Jesus knows what it is like when God's wonderful peace fills our hearts. At these times we get the impression that now all is well. We have encountered Jesus. Our lives belong to Him. We belong to His congregation. Filled and enraptured with this gift of God we think we are close to Him and love Him. We are certain that now nothing adverse can happen to us.

But then comes the inevitable, which under all circumstances must come: the next step! Jesus says to us, "We must go on! I have set the table for you in the presence of your enemies. You have eaten and drunk; I have strengthened you. Now we must go further!"

Day 31

SETTING OUT FOR THE DESERT

Being saved, receiving forgiveness and salvation, is only the bread which gives us strength to set out for the desert, towards our mountain of God where we will in truth encounter God and ourselves. The desert is not always an external reality but is usually an inner condition of our souls, a period of darkness and drought. In the desert God will ask us about our deepest motives. He will reveal His heart to us. He will call us to follow after His Son in order to transform us into His image. Up till now we had not even been disciples! We had merely been guests at Jesus' table. He nourished us and relieved us of our burdens. And while we are still sitting at the table, we are challenged to set out, as we read, "Then Jesus was led by the Spirit into the desert" (Matthew 4:1).

This is where the path to discipleship begins, for discipleship means following after Jesus on His path. Jesus says of Himself,

> "Foxes have holes and birds of the air have nests, but the Son of Man has nowhere to lay his head."
>
> (Luke 9:58)

And of His disciples He says,

"If anyone would come after me, he must deny himself and take up his cross and follow me."

(Matthew 16:24)

Jesus forces no one to be His disciple. But if we want to follow Him He cannot spare us the confrontation with ourselves and with the conditions of discipleship. In the desert God reveals the true condition of our hearts. The Holy Spirit must lead us deeper into truth. The desert begins to gnaw at us. We get hungry and thirsty. Our senses cry out for satisfaction, for peace, even for numbness.

But in the desert God doesn't respond to our cries. He seems silent, unmoved by our need. Because our longing for comfort, joy, peace and security is not stilled, the dams of suppression begin to burst. Our inner being surfaces. Suppressed emptiness, existential fears, feelings of inferiority, self-rejection, loneliness, bitterness, accusations and anger erupt out of a seething heart and clog the mouth with bitter gall.

In the desert all the hitherto locked inner rooms are unbolted. Nothing can remain hidden. The light must shine into every dark corner so that the truth can penetrate and transform our hearts. In His goodness, God continues to lead us ever deeper into the desert during the course of our discipleship. This reveals the mystery of our transformation into the image of His Son. None of us could bear the knowledge of our heart's need of salvation if it were revealed all at once.

Day 32

SEPARATING THE CHAFF
FROM THE WHEAT

Our initial reaction to this process is usually confusion, disappointment and doubt. We don't understand what is happening. The familiar peace has evaporated. We no longer understand God; His Word no longer speaks to us as once it did. We have the impression that we are suddenly much worse off than before we lived with Jesus.

The Spirit also led Jesus into the desert. These desert periods always initiate an encounter with God in which He wants to engrave the mysteries of His kingdom deeper into our hearts. Without these desert phases we will never really know the condition of our relationship with Jesus, or how serious we are about discipleship. The desert is absolutely necessary in order for God's Spirit to lead us into truth. The Holy Spirit is the one who reveals Jesus to us; He must therefore lead us into the desert, into our personal desert.

The wilderness is the place where God's wind sweeps away all the chaff and straw, all void and meaninglessness, all noise and numbness, exposing the bare foundation. The illusions and day-dreams with which we covered up our wretched reality dissolve painfully before our heart's burning eyes. Even God's loving care, which used to fill us during times of praise, when we read His Word, when we were quiet in His presence, or in the fellowship of friends and other believers (yes, this sometimes intoxicated us like a good book or film, or whatever else we used for relaxation) is taken from us. It recedes so far that we lose all appetite for it.

There are periods in our lives when too many emotions, even in our relationship with God, can distract us from the essential work on our hearts. For the sake of the truth, God must hold Himself back. He must bring us to the place where at last everything which was in our hearts is revealed and where we experience the truth about ourselves; to the place where no further suppression is possible, no further distraction is effective – whether religion, hedonism or culture. We know, after all, that God's enemy is not choosy about the means he employs to prevent us from experiencing the truth about ourselves and about God. This makes the desert absolutely necessary.

Day 33

ENCOUNTER WITH MY TRUE SELF

When we look into our own eyes in the desert, we will encounter our true self. This self is normally filled with self-rejection and with accusations against our own personal history because fear, insecurity and homelessness dominate our lives. Rebellion against the path God gave us is the usual reaction in this place. It appears to us like a chronic illness. Only then do we begin to sense our heart's incredible need of salvation. We discover how quickly we mistrust God and turn from Him when things don't develop as we had expected. Then God must expose us to the enemy's attacks in order to reveal the true state of our relationship to Him.

On the one hand, the desert is a fruitless wilderness of solitude and homelessness, where an unprotected, solitary person is constantly surrounded by death. Therefore it is the home of demons and the devil is very present. On the other hand, the same desert can be a jewel of beauty and a sea of peace and glory when God's breath fills it with His whisperings, when He lays hold of the unplumbed depths of our soul. God speaks and acts in the desert. God's Spirit led Jesus into the desert and exposed Him to the attacks, the questions and above all the lies of the devil.

This method is necessary in order to prepare and equip us, because the path of discipleship will take us through a world ruled by God's enemy. We must go to the desert to learn the difference between God's voice and the devil's. The wilderness is the training arena, where God's Spirit familiarizes me with the strategy of "the liar and accuser of the brethren." He teaches me to recognize the devil's wiles. I learn to differentiate between lies and truth, light and darkness, pride and humility. Then I can see Jesus' footprints and stay on the path in a world marked by deception and pride.

Day 34

THE TEST

What do we usually experience in the desert? Our first impression, as we have observed, is that God has abandoned us, because we no longer feel Him or hear His voice. We lose our desire to pray and read God's Word. Everything in and around us is empty and dull. The needs of our soul and our spirit are no longer satisfied. We no longer feel peace. Our spiritual life is dehydrated and everything is tasteless. Love for God becomes purely an act of the will. It no longer elevates us.

If we don't cover up and whitewash this condition with a façade of activities and consumerism, but allow our heart to speak, the cracks in the walls of our inner dams will begin to appear. The negative things in our heart surface. Accusations, disappointment, anger and resignation will spread.

Then the devil comes and says, "You see, your conversion, your so-called experiences with God are nothing but religious emotionalism. You just fell for what people said." The enemy knows how to target his lies according to where we are currently at in our relationship to God. He says, "Look, there's no solution for your present situation! God may be a God who heals, but you aren't on His list. He doesn't see you. God heals and liberates, but you're so wounded and imprisoned, your past is so difficult that there's little hope."

The devil doesn't say that God doesn't heal, that He doesn't intervene or that He isn't present. He only says, "You're a special case! God can help, but there are certain cases even He can't solve and you're one of them. Your case is more complicated than others." Lying is the devil's weapon. He comes and tells us, "You have to learn to live with your situation. You must accept that this is the way you are and you can't change yourself in this situation. It's just a shortcoming in your character that you can't open up to others and that it's hard for you to let others see into your heart. Not much can be done about this. This is easier for some people." In this way the devil begins wrapping us up in lies. His goal in the desert is that we see ourselves as victims – victims of God's demands and calling or victims of our past, our upbringing or other circumstances. He wants us to feel sorry for ourselves because then we won't take responsibility or give account for our thoughts and actions. We will experience neither repentance nor forgiveness and a new beginning.

Day 35

THE DEVIL'S WHISPERING

The enemy of God and man always approaches us at our weak point. He drags us down by converting our weaknesses into paralysis. Whatever our weaknesses – self-pity, lack of courage, resignation, fear or mistrust – if we don't put them in God's hands, the devil will always be able to use them as weapons against us. In our struggle for genuine discipleship Satan will always pressurize us with the lie that radical discipleship and total openness and honesty are only for saints, not for the weak. A John Smith like myself must not overdo it. We need only read books about saints. What they went through is not for people with little strength of character. This perseverance is much more than you and I could muster in order to fulfill the radical demands of discipleship, which in fact is a matter of relinquishing our own goals and dreams. It's a matter of a life without guarantee of visible success, recognition or security; without hope for an empire of our own, however small.

Day 36

WHAT MAY IT COST?

God allows temptation. When our heart is revealed we must ask ourselves whether we are willing to believe God's Word and His promises – namely that He will lead us into life through darkness, problems and struggles if we lay our lives in His hands. When it comes to letting go of our own lives, rebellion, lack of faith, pride, feelings of inferiority, fear and cowardice can rear up like an impenetrable wall between us and God. At this decisive point He asks us, "Are you really ready to follow after Me, even when it costs you everything? Are you willing, even if I don't always give you pleasure, if you have to pass through times of dryness and darkness, if things don't always go well? Even if you lose a child, your spouse or your friends? Are you then still willing to follow Me for My sake? Or do you follow Me only as long as I fulfill your desires?"

Love for God is a relationship, born of the unconditional decision to belong to Him, anchored in the heart attitude described in Psalm 73:25,

> "Whom have I in heaven but you? And earth has nothing I desire besides you."

Love is decision, whether our desires are fulfilled or not. It is a matter of seeking God as a person, rather than His riches or His gifts. The desert makes it plain whether we live from the world's nourishment or from God's Word. God seeks our total dedication. He wants to be our sole source of life.

Dedication is saying yes to God's paths in spite of all opposition. "Lord, I want to go with You. I trust You that You really are who You say You are in Your Word. You are life, You are love – therefore I will give myself up into Your hands. You will bear me in my pain, my emptiness, my fear, my despair over myself. You will bring me to the goal."

Day 37

LEARNING TO FIGHT

In the desert God teaches us to fight the true battle against the enemy. He teaches us to overcome the devil by the only strategy which really leads to the goal. The first point is: "the blood of the Lamb." Here we must do nothing. Jesus has shed His blood. If in the desert the devil accuses us, "Just see how your heart looks, how broken, guilty and impossible you are. You don't have a chance..." then we can say, "It's true, I'm guilty, I'm weak. [It's best to confront the devil with truth, which he can't stand.] But the blood of the Lamb cleanses me. And there's nothing in this creation which can resist the blood of Jesus. There's nothing in my heart which can't be cleansed by the blood of the Lamb. No guilt is so great – neither in my life nor among the nations – that it can't be forgiven through the blood of God's Lamb."

This silences the enemy. If we really believe that the blood of the Lamb is stronger than every embedded characteristic in our lives, stronger than every ethnic characteristic, every tradition and every other power, we need not fear the enemy's accusations. In desert periods, the meaning of the Lamb's blood becomes truly precious. It is the sole means by which we can stand up to the enemy.

Day 38

THE WORD OF TESTIMONY

The second point in the overcomer strategy is: "the word of testimony." What does this mean? It is the testimony that Jesus overcame everything on the cross. In the desert everything points to the cross. In the wilderness we experience the truth and reality of the cross for our lives. There God shows us how incurably sick our hearts have become through separation from Him who is life; how pride, arrogance, lies and greed hold us imprisoned in a hopeless condition; how un-whole, confused and destroyed our lives are, so that we can only cry out like Paul, "What a wretched man I am! Who will rescue me...?" (Romans 7:24). But together with the depth of our need for salvation, He also reveals the liberating message which makes possible hope and the restoration of our personality. On the cross Jesus bore not only our guilt, but also the sickness of our humanity, the pain, the isolation and confusion of our soul, the wounds and deep grooves of destruction caused by our own history. He took on Himself the crushing burden which was on our shoulders, the deadly poison in our hearts, the deep depression in our spirits. He wants us to stand up, breathe, hope, be joyful and live.

There is nothing in our lives which Jesus cannot liberate and lead into freedom and life. He who knows us to the depths of our souls is wholly for us. God is love and we were created for Him. What a message! When this testimony lives in our hearts and we confess it before the visible and the invisible world, the enemy of God, the enemy of life, must yield.

Day 39

NOT LOVING LIFE SO MUCH
AS TO SHRINK FROM DEATH

The third part of the overcomer strategy is: "they did not love their lives so much as to shrink from death" (Revelation 12:11b). This refers not only to those who long for martyrdom, but to every person who begins following Jesus. This is not just one last heroic deed when, for example, we are thrown into prison somewhere to die; it is the willingness to let go of our lives daily, one small, painful piece at a time. Paul said,

> "For your sake we face death all day long; we are considered as sheep to be slaughtered."
>
> (Romans 8:36)

This is a daily dying for Jesus' sake; we let go of our lives in installments.

If we confess Jesus in our lives and in this world, we will certainly make ourselves vulnerable to attack, because we live in a world which is hostile to Jesus. Whoever fears for his life is easy prey for the devil because he can be blackmailed with threats and violence. If we are afraid to lose our lives, we are easy to overcome. Only those who have no fear of losing their lives have nothing to fear from the devil.

God wants to teach us how we can overcome the enemy: through the blood of the Lamb, through the word of our testimony and by not loving our lives so much as to cringe from death. All of this begins in the desert. If someone who is reading this finds himself in the desert right now, he may know that nothing better can happen to him because he is in a place where his love for Jesus will gain authenticity, substance and truth. In the desert we draw closer to Jesus and experience who He really is.

Day 40

SELF-PITY OR FULLNESS OF LIFE

It is important that we do not rebel in the desert, but watch and pray so that we can know the difference between Jesus' voice and the enemy's. This protects us from falling into a victim mentality. The enemy always sides with our self-pity. He sides with our rebellion. He sides with our distaste for suffering and declares, "Yes, of course, this shouldn't happen to you. God is asking too much when He put you in such a situation. This is impossible. It contradicts God's love. Do something to end this situation as quickly as possible." The devil's voice is always very much on the side of our problems! But God's voice asks, "Do you love Me, even in this situation? Are you standing with Me? Are you really willing to persevere with Me even if you receive no answer now? Are you willing to be completely open? May I give you a heart of flesh, which is a vulnerable heart?"

Jesus' words, "I have come that they may have life, and have it to the full" (John 10:10b) are always a banner above God's work in us. Yes, we can experience fullness of life in the desert, for after Jesus was tempted there, "angels came and attended him" (Matthew 4:11). Every one of us can experience that. If Jesus' love penetrates our hearts, if we have given Him our "Yes" and have continued with Him, we will experience an increasingly full life. Then angels will really serve us in His name.

Section 5

DO YOU LOVE ME?

And we know that in all things God works for the
good of those who love him...

(Romans 8:28)

Day 41

GOD IS NOT A SCHOOLMASTER

In John 21:15-17 Jesus asks Simon Peter three times in a row, "Simon, do you love Me?" We could ask ourselves why Jesus even asked him this. After all, He always knows what is in our hearts. So why this question? It's understandable when we humans ask one another such questions. We can't see into each other's hearts and thus are often unsure of the other's motives in relationships and actions. But of God it is said, "You know me to the bottom of my soul" (Psalm 139:15 [translation of German version]). And yet Jesus asks us, "Do you love Me?" This is not a rhetorical question and I am convinced that Jesus does not want to set us a trap. He neither wants to test us nor expose our powerlessness and weakness. Jesus doesn't want to drive us into a corner. When He stands before us asking this question, we must be careful not to give a superficial answer, or say the correct words without thinking.

Jesus asks us this question because He is so concerned about our lives. He cares about us as Lord and friend. We often have the impression that when Jesus turns to us, it is primarily because He wants us to do something for Him. We think He's coming like the owner of the vineyard in order to check up on us and count how many baskets we filled today. Deep in our hearts we still picture God as the omnipresent schoolmaster standing behind us with his notebook, registering everything we have done wrong. That is why we can so easily misunderstand God.

Day 42

SERVING GOD DOES NOT NECESSARILY MEAN LOVING GOD

The question about our love is not intended to control us. It is much more an expression of His concern. We read in 1 Peter 5:7,

> Cast all your anxiety on him because he cares for you.

Jesus' question aims primarily to ensure our well-being. "We know that in all things God works for the good of those who love him" (Romans 8:28). However, not everything that happens to us automatically serves our good just because we have placed our lives in God's service – whether in active involvement in a congregation, in home or foreign missions, in generous financial support of Christian work and the needy, or whatever else we can catalogue. For it says, "all things work for the good of those who love him."

That is why Jesus' question "Do you love Me?" is so important existentially. He wants everything we encounter in daily life to really work for our good, i.e. for life, for joy, for freedom, for peace, for fulfillment – because God cares for us. Jesus asks you and me about our love for Him. He does this several times a day in order to give us opportunities to be aware of where our heart is taking us. Where am I actually going? What is my everyday life like? Are all my acts, thoughts and words aligned with Jesus, from my heart? Do I really keep Him holy? Does whatever I'm saying, doing and thinking right now honor Him? Do my actions express my love for Him? Where have I left the path of love, where have I lost sight of Jesus?

Day 43

GOD WANTS OUR ATTENTION

We can easily stray from the right path because, according to God's Word, by nature we human beings are like sheep. Sheep often go astray and get lost if they aren't being led and protected by a shepherd. The prophet Isaiah says,

> We all, like sheep, have gone astray,
> each of us has turned to his own way;
> and the Lord has laid on him the iniquity of us all.
>
> (Isaiah 53:6)

Our own paths are always godless and end in guilt. Jesus does not want us to become guilty, for guilt makes our lives dark and cold. Therefore He asks us daily, "Do you love Me?" It is a question designed to call us back, realign us, awaken us and speak to us; a question to arrest us in our routine, in our thoughtlessness, superficiality and repression; a question to bring us out of our self-confidence, self-overestimation or self-pity. Jesus wants to tell us, "My son, My daughter, wake up! I want to talk to you."

When our daughter Hanna was a small child she developed a simple but highly successful tactic to gain my full attention in order to tell me something. She just took my face in her hands and turned it toward her so that I had to look at her. Only then did she share what was on her mind. This is exactly what Jesus does with His question. He wants to turn our faces to Him so that we look into His eyes. Then He says, "Do you know whom you belong to? Do you know where you're at home? Do you realize that you are wholly surrounded by Me – at this moment and all day, wherever you go and whatever your situation? It is written, 'You hem me in – behind and before; you have laid your hand upon me' (Psalm 139:5). Are you aware of this? Do you really believe this – right now, at this moment? Do you love Me? You have so little joy, so little peace. Look into My face. In My Word it is written, 'Those who look to him are radiant' [German 'with joy'] (Psalm 34:5)."

Day 44

THE RIGHT LOOK

Looking at Jesus – not just briefly in our personal quiet time in the morning, but as a constant heart attitude – means knowing that our face and our heart are in His hands. If we don't look at Jesus' face over and over again during the day, we shouldn't be surprised if there is little joy in our daily lives. The path to joy is given: "Those who look to him are radiant [with joy]" (Psalm 34:5). Many of us go through our days like Cain – with a downcast face. God said to him, "If you do what is right [i.e. if your heart is free], you can look up at Me. If you do not do what is right [i.e. if your heart is bound to the things of this world], sin is crouching at your door; it desires to have you" (cf. Genesis 4:7). Lifting our eyes means looking into God's face because our heart is free and directed to Him. If we look at the ground we're not aligned with God, but something else drives us, pushes us down and imprisons us.

"Do you love Me?" – If we let Jesus repeat this question every day, it will keep renewing our eyes, our path and our heart attitude to God. It will illuminate our relationship to ourselves, to our brothers and sisters, to the world and to everything we do. Jesus' question affects the source, goal and center of our being, reminding us of Colossians 3:23-24,

Whatever you do, work at it with all your heart, as working for the Lord, not for men, since you know that you will receive an inheritance from the Lord as a reward.

Doing everything for Jesus means always looking into His face. In Psalm 18 we see a person who from his whole heart kept God before him and looked into His face. Characteristically the psalm begins with the words,

I love you, O Lord, my strength.
The Lord is my rock, my fortress and my deliverer;
my God is my rock, in whom I take refuge.
He is my shield and the horn of my salvation, my stronghold.
I call to the Lord, who is worthy of praise,
and I am saved from my enemies.

The psalmist can hardly stop describing everything God is to him. A powerful torrent of joy, enthusiasm and trust pours from his heart because he is looking into God's face. "I love you, O Lord, my strength!"

Day 45

DAVID'S SECRET

Of course, we quickly conclude that it was easy for the psalmist David to speak as he does in Psalm 18. After all, he was one of God's favorites. But we, on the other hand – the rank and file who must cook with ordinary water – have little reason or opportunity for such exuberance and passion. We are pressured by so many fears and adversities that we have our hands full with the daily battle for spiritual survival. We're left with little room for fervency and effervescence. David had it easy; God was close to him.

And that is true. God was close to David, very close. But this does not alter the fact that in the same Psalm 18 David cries out,

> The cords of death entangled me;
> the torrents of destruction overwhelmed me.
> The cords of the grave coiled around me;
> the snares of death confronted me.
>
> (vv. 4-5)

David was no stranger to temptations, suffering and the impression that God was distant. On the contrary, the depth and quality of his faith were formed in just these times of suffering in the desert and darkness, as we see in many of his psalms.

In Psalm 13 David cried to God,

How long, O Lord? Will you forget me for ever?
How long will you hide your face from me?
How long must I wrestle with my thoughts and
every day have sorrow in my heart?

(vv. 1-2)

David, chosen by God to be king of Israel one day, had
first to spend part of his life as a refugee and servant of
the godless, despised Philistines in order to survive (see
1 Samuel 27). David would have had many significant
reasons to doubt both his calling and God's presence and
care. But we see his greatness precisely when in the midst
of his problems he could say,

In my distress I called to the Lord;
I cried to my God for help.
From his temple he heard my voice;
my cry came before him, into his ears.

(Psalm 18:6)

Instead of leaving God's presence in times of doubts and
accusations, David flung himself onto Him. He knew that
God was for him, no matter what his present situation was
like. In Psalm 73 he prayed with Asaph,

Whom have I in heaven but you?
And earth has nothing I desire besides you.
My flesh and my heart may fail,
but God is the strength of my heart and my portion forever.

(vv. 25-26)

Day 46

THROWING OURSELVES ON GOD

David understood that the living God of Israel was the sole source of hope, help, comfort, peace and joy. Therefore with the passion of despair he threw his whole existence on God; not even storms, quakes and darkness could shake him off. He knew that all paths which do not lead to God's heart would end in despair; that all cries not directed to his God's ear would echo emptily; that all looks not directed to his God would be lost in darkness. That is why – after he had cried out to his God in need and pain, holding fast to him – he could confidently confess,

> He brought me out into a spacious place;
> he rescued me because he delighted in me.
>
> (Psalm 18:19)

David's outstanding characteristic was his unreserved surrender to God's love. He made that love the foundation of his life, the core of his identity, the source of his security and freedom, the place of his peace, the power of his actions. The awareness of being loved by God was so important and ever-present that nothing could darken God's countenance for David. Nothing could rob him of the faith that God is good and repays those who seek Him. "My cry will come before him, for he loves me!" This is the faith which makes us into men and women after God's heart: God is love and we are created for Him... God is absolutely good and our lives are in His hands in every situation... Nothing and no one can tear us out of God's hands – not even sin...

David actually fell into very great sin. He committed adultery and murder. How could a person with such guilt still be called "a man after God's heart" (cf. Acts 13:22)? David's secret did not lie in his moral fortitude or his gifts, but in his heart attitude. When Nathan the prophet confronted him with his offence, King David did not consider himself too good to humble himself before God and the people, and to accept the consequences without complaint. His guilt and repentance were made public and even today every child can learn about it. For David there was no alternative. He knew not only that God is greater than all guilt, but also that there is no other hope for anyone than to go to God with the guilt, no matter how grave it is. As the psalmist said,

> If you, O Lord, kept a record of sins,
> O Lord, who could stand?

> (Psalm 130:3)

David never lost his faith in God's goodness, love and holiness even in the despair caused by his sin. His repentance was thus a deep brokenness in the eyes of the whole world.

Day 47

FRUIT OF REPENTANCE

The depth of brokenness and repentance in a person's life corresponds to the depth of restoration and the newly awakened authority. The fact that we men and women of God can fall into sin is really not surprising, for sin is always lurking outside our door. It entices and tempts us in our weak moments. If we do not fall, this is solely due to our Lord's mercy. But our heart's quality is truly revealed only by the depth of our brokenness, by the genuineness and fruits of our repentance and by the depth of our disgust over the sin we tasted. That is why David was still called "a man after God's heart" even after his great sin – or then all the more!

The same is true of Peter, who wept bitterly over his betrayal of Jesus and hid his guilt from no one. He found his way back to the heart of his Lord – who restored him, as a man after His own heart, as leader of the apostles. Whoever has truly aligned his heart with his God cannot be driven away through sin and weakness. And God in His faithfulness will transform even guilt and weakness into good – the very best – for the person who clings to Him and does not doubt His love.

Day 48

GOD PROTECTS OUR HEART

Those who do not really know God's love in His Son Jesus nor truly love Him in return can easily fall apart when guilt, weakness and problems are suddenly poured over them in a deluge, for the depths of their hearts are not directed to God but to circumstances and to themselves. They know neither hope nor help, like Judas who hanged himself after his betrayal because he was not aligned with Jesus and had not really known Jesus' heart. Thus, in his need and guilt he couldn't find the way to Jesus' heart in order to receive forgiveness. Judas hanged himself. Others turn away from God because they persuade themselves, "Now it's over. No one can help me any more."

Neither could King Saul find the way back to God's heart because he did not look into God's countenance. Saul was primarily concerned with attaining his military goals; he strove to preserve his authority and save face. Of course he wanted to serve God and the people with these goals, but on his conditions and with his methods. Because his eyes and heart were focused on himself he broke down under pressure and ended up committing suicide. He actually thought that all would be lost if his people and his soldiers deserted him. He disobeyed God because he didn't really count on Him. So God was unable to use Saul's difficult situation for his best.

How God wishes we were so aligned with Him that nothing could ever alarm or trouble us because we know that everything we encounter must serve for our best. Let us have Jesus remind us, re-orient us and ask us daily, "Do you love Me? Are you looking into My face? Do you believe that I love you? Do you allow My Word to mold you? Are you certain that your complaints reach My ears? Do you believe that I hear you?"

Let us expose ourselves to God's message for our lives.

> "For I know the plans I have for you," declares the Lord, "plans to prosper you and not to harm you, plans to give you hope and a future."
>
> (Jeremiah 29:11)

God's thoughts must spread out in our heart and become like a protective layer which makes it indestructible. It is indestructible because it is so secure in God's love, goodness and mercy that evil, fear and darkness can no longer reach there.

Day 49

DAILY PRACTICE

The daily practice of gazing trustfully into His countenance is not a matter of five minutes' quiet time per day. It is not a duty but a continuing conversation. It's a dialogue between two loving hearts who have much to say to each other every day. Jesus wants to direct our faces toward Himself so that we can radiate joy. This is not a question of a method but of our determination. Do we give credence to God's thoughts about us? Can we say from our hearts, "I want Him to be in everything I do because He is my love and the center of my being. I want to know Him deeper every day and sacrifice everything for His sake"?

If we really love, we will happily read our beloved's letters over and over again. I have letters from my wife which she wrote me more than twenty-six years ago and I still enjoy reading them, even though what she wrote is – thank God for it – the same as she writes today. But I now understand it more deeply because our love has grown; it has become part of our lives and has stood the test. If we really love Jesus we will go to Him over and over again, saying, "Lord, please tell me again how You see me. And I, too, will tell You over and over again that I love You."

Friends, read the letter of your Beloved, read God's Word! Memorize it! See to it that His Word accompanies you, surrounds you, pursues you. May His Word dwell in us in such a way that our hearts – even if we are old or ill and have no more energy to read it actively – become springs from which God's words flow like a living, healing stream. There will be situations in our lives when the only things we can fall back on will be what is engraved on our hearts, as on a CD.

Just think how lovely it is to listen to old people who love Jesus and can effortlessly quote God's Word from their hearts. This is like distributing precious treasures from a treasure box. Because these people exposed themselves to God's message, the mystery was able to unfold in their hearts. "Your face will be radiant with joy because all things work for the best of those who love him" (cf. Psalm 34:6 and Romans 8:28).

Section 6

THROUGH STORMS TO THE GOAL

One day Jesus said to his disciples, "Let's go over
to the other side of the lake." So they got into a
boat and set out. As they sailed, he fell asleep. A
squall came down on the lake, so that the boat
was being swamped, and they were in great
danger. The disciples went and woke him, saying,
"Master, Master, we're going to drown!" He got
up and rebuked the wind and the raging waters;
the storm subsided, and all was calm. "Where
is your faith?" he asked his disciples. In fear and
amazement they asked one another, "Who is this?
He commands even the winds and the water, and
they obey him."

(Luke 8:22-25)

Day 50

GOING TO THE OTHER SHORE

This report of a storm on the Sea of Galilee is an impressive story, even though it may be difficult for us to picture how there could have been such strong waves on this relatively small lake. But I have been told that the wind there really can produce alarming conditions. So I can imagine that the small fishing boats of those days were tossed around like walnut shells and could easily have capsized. It's also possible that the disciples couldn't swim.

In any case, Jesus' instructions were clear. He told His disciples, "Get into the boat. We're going to the other side." Then He fell asleep and the boat ran into a severe storm. It was so dangerous that even these experienced fishermen feared for their lives. They cried out, "We'll be destroyed! We're drowning!"

If we look at this story more closely we realize that their words are still very relevant for us. This is first of all a story about discipleship. Just as Jesus called the disciples, He calls us today to come and get into "His boat." He also tells us the goal, "Let's go to the shore on the other side." When Jesus calls us, He always gives us a goal. In God's kingdom there is no such thing as lack of purpose or direction. And where there is a goal, there is also a route. Jesus sends us on this route. "Get into the boat and cross the water to the other side."

Day 51

LETTING GO OF THE RUDDER

It is no coincidence that the route leads over water. We know what water symbolizes. It is not man's element. Without help and protection, he cannot survive long in it. It not only engulfs us, but it is also filled with mysterious creatures. And Jesus says, "Go across the water to the other shore." This journey can be traveled only by boat. It's impossible to run across, as we can on land which gives us the feeling that we can determine our own steps. In a boat we are at the mercy of the navigator's guidance.

Jesus sends us out on the water in order to reach the goal He has in mind for us. This is a route that is not under our control. If we want to be honest, we actually never have control over our lives – no matter how much we want and strive for it with all possible means. But we cannot determine whether we will fall ill, how long we will live or when we will die… Of course a person can end his life. But if he thinks he can thus escape from himself and his creator, he will have a rude awakening. The Bible says, "God cannot be mocked. A man reaps what he sows" (Galatians 6:7).

Day 52

WE CANNOT INSURE EVERYTHING

There are things in our lives which we ultimately cannot greatly influence. Humans are simply at the mercy of many eventualities. Even if we are alert we cannot, for example, prevent an irresponsible person (who has perhaps drunk too much) from one day losing control over his car and running us down. There's nothing we can do about this, and the feeling of being at someone else's mercy frightens us. Yes, in this world man is on his own. He is at the mercy of all those forces which can destroy life.

We can write many books about life. We can think up theories and formulas for safeguarding ourselves. But in the end we must admit that we do not have our lives in our own hands. We know Jesus' story of the rich farmer who thought he could get his life under control. So he built a huge barn and filled it with grain, i.e. with wealth, pleasure, enjoyment, health and whatever else we think of in connection with a pleasant and secure life. Then he said to himself, "Now, my soul, you can enjoy life." In other words, "I have rid myself of all insecurity, all pressure, all worries – now I can be happy." And what does God say to him? "You fool! This very night you will die" (see Luke 12:16-21).

What good are all our safeguards? Do we think they give us control over our lives? Many try to sell us some form of security. We Swiss are very familiar with this phenomenon.

Why are there so many insurance companies in Switzerland? I think it is because we want to safeguard at least some aspect of life. Being exposed and afraid are existential realities for mankind. We fear illness, loneliness, failure, not being loved, wounds, pain, war and catastrophes. Ultimately we are afraid of death because it is the moment when we definitely lose control. It is the moment we must let go of everything because it simply falls out of our hands.

Woe to the person who plunges into a dark abyss because in his heart he does not know about God's loving hands that hold us, saying, "Good and faithful servant, enter into your master's joy" (see Matthew 25:21). I think there can be no greater terror than for a person to realize at death what it really means to be lost and at another's mercy. This fear is so real that Jesus said, "In this world you will have trouble. [Many German translations read, 'you will have fear.'] But take heart! I have overcome the world" (John 16:33).

Fear and being at others' mercy are characteristics of a godless world – a world which does not know God at all, or insufficiently. External fear attacks us in terrifying forms and images, which have their origin in our own unsaved lives, always telling us the same thing, "You're lost! You have no future!"

Day 53

BEING SHAKEN

Jesus sent His disciples across the lake with a goal. It is important to keep in mind that this story is about Jesus' disciples who entrusted themselves to Him. He sits in the boat with them and says, "Go over to the shore on the other side." Jesus gives all His disciples a goal – a common goal. He says, "Get into the boat and I will bring you over into life, into My kingdom, into your life's fulfillment." That is the great destination.

But along the way there are many sub-goals – a calling or different tasks and phases within a calling to which Jesus calls us individually, saying, "Come, get in here, I am with you." And even when we set out for the goal in faith and in obedience to His words, we encounter hurdles, difficulties and sometimes impossibilities. We go through storms and are shaken, and Jesus does not prevent it. He spares us neither the threat nor the fear. How else could we ever grasp the meaning of the words, "Even though I walk through the valley of the shadow of death, I will fear no evil, for you are with me; your rod and your staff, they comfort me" (Psalm 23:4)? Only a person who has experienced God's firm hands and the shepherd's comfort in such darkness will be fully released from existential fear and made capable of living.

Day 54

IN THE PRESENCE OF OUR ENEMIES

We often have the impression that when we follow Jesus, serve Him and obey Him we will be shielded from pain, trouble and suffering. At least He should see that we don't fall ill, that our families are free of accidents, that we don't get into trouble or fail. But Jesus does not always act according to our notions. He seems to have a different view of things and of our lives. Then we can become very disappointed – because we misunderstand Him. We always tend to seek external security, but Jesus' goal is to lead us to fulfillment and to His destination – not ours. Our goal is always to reach Paradise as quickly and easily as possible, without pain and suffering. But that is not God's goal.

God's purpose is that in this world we experience His presence in the darkness, in the midst of the storm and all the powers which surround us. He is Lord over life and death. He is Lord over all the powers around us. He is also Lord over our fear. We read of Him in Colossians 2:15 that He disarmed the powers and authorities. And He wants us to experience this. His goal is that we know Him, not that we get through life unscathed because we serve Him.

Luke's account of the storm reminds us of a story about Peter in Matthew 14:22-33. As Jesus is walking on the water toward the disciples, He challenges Peter, "Come on the water, come to me!" Peter takes up the challenge, only to experience that Jesus does not prevent a giant wave from approaching. Jesus must have known that this would frighten Peter. But He doesn't prevent it. Peter should experience that Jesus is Lord over heaven and earth, Lord of the natural laws and the destructive powers which reign over this world and which man is exposed to.

Jesus wants so much for us to know who He is. But where would we learn this if not in the situation where He conquers these powers in front of our eyes – these powers which want to enslave our spirit and our soul? We would prefer not to have to come anywhere near these powers any more. But on the path with Him Jesus does not prevent us from being shaken. It doesn't say in Psalm 23, "You prepare a table before me in the absence of my enemies," but "You prepare a table before me in the presence of my enemies" (v. 5). When we look into the eyes of our enemies, i.e. our problems – no matter how fearsome they may be – He prepares a table for us right in their presence.

Day 55

WHERE IS YOUR FAITH?

Back to the story of the storm. We read that the disciples began to cry out with fear. They probably scrambled to bail the water out of the boat. The way I appraise Peter, he grabbed the nearest pail and called to the others, "Come on and help bail water!" But when he and the others realized that they couldn't control the situation they went to Jesus. This is what I admire about Peter. In the end he always saw where he could get help. Even when he was sinking he didn't lose hope, but called out to his Lord, "Lord, help me!"

The disciples' cry for help is not without a reproach, "Wake up, Jesus, how can You sleep while we're going under?" When we're in trouble, don't we, too, often have the feeling that Jesus is sleeping? Or that He isn't interested in our situation? He doesn't even seem to notice that we're going under. How often have we thought this and thrown around the "why" questions? Why don't You answer? Why are You so far away? Why have You abandoned me? Why don't You help me? In short, why are You sleeping? These questions often become accusations. "Teacher, don't you care if we drown?" (Mark 4:38). "Are You indifferent to my lot? I'm about to go under and it's Your fault because You aren't intervening!"

The disciples also went to Jesus with this accusation. Jesus' reaction revealed His painful disappointment at how little they knew His heart and His authority. Thank God that they came to Him. But that wasn't enough. Jesus said, "Where is your faith?" We could put it another way, "Do you know so little about Me? Have you still not understood who I am?"

We must not forget that the disciples got into the boat shortly after they had seen Jesus feed 5,000 people with a few fish and pieces of bread. They had just seen that He was Lord over natural laws. Now a strong wind and high waves are enough to make them forget everything! What saddens Jesus is the fact that we so often and so quickly misunderstand Him and think He could actually abandon us. But He says to us, "How could I be indifferent about you? I gave My life for you!? Where is your faith?" We must hold on to one thing: Jesus brings us to the goal! Every person who gets into the boat with Jesus in order to go over to the other shore will reach the goal, even if there are storms on the way. Jesus wants His image to crystallize in our hearts while we are crossing over this lake; He wants our faith and our trust to grow.

Jesus wants us to know Him more and more deeply and to see how He overcomes life-threatening situations. He, the Lord of the universe, calls to us, "Come to Me, you who are driven, who are burdened with fears and doubts. I want to give you rest." He waits for our profession of trust and faith, "Lord, I know You're bringing me to the goal. I know that nothing can happen to me which does not serve for my best. I know that everything I encounter must first pass through Your loving heart. Give me strength to wait for You to act. You won't desert me!" And Jesus will answer, "I'm here. Be comforted! Trust Me. Relax. I am Lord of the situation."

TRUSTING LIKE A CHILD

In 1 John 4:18 we read, "There is no fear in love. But perfect love drives out fear." The deeper our heart comprehends what love God expresses in His Son Jesus, the more fear will loosen its grip on our lives. Trust, relaxation and peace are part of our inheritance on the trip to the other shore! What we need is childlike trust. "If God is for us, who can be against us?" (Romans 8:31). A person with childlike trust will certainly reach the destination because he knows that his heavenly Father is absolutely on his side. This is the Father who sent His beloved Son into the deepest darkness in order to liberate and save. Jesus makes unmistakably clear that we can neither understand nor reach God's goals if we don't have the same uncomplicated trust in Him that little children have. It is that same heart attitude which Jesus Himself had to the Father. He could say, "Father, I know that You always hear me" (cf. John 11:42). He knew He could encounter nothing which did not first pass through the Father. And the Father never sleeps, not even for a moment:

indeed, he who watches over Israel
will neither slumber nor sleep.

(Psalm 121:4)

Getting into the boat with Jesus and crossing over the lake means that we will undoubtedly have an adventurous life. Life with Jesus is an adventure because there are many storms to survive. Paul says of those who follow Jesus, "We must go through many hardships to enter the kingdom of God" (Acts 14:22). No one will be spared this. Why? So that we can learn that we really have no reason to fear. The powers have been overcome; they cannot injure the core of our lives. They can shake us like grain, which ultimately serves only to free us from the chaff. But that does not destroy us.

So when our desire for security sounds an alarm because the storms and fears grow ominous, we can hold fast to the fact that our boat will not capsize. God will bring us to the goal. Of that there can be no shadow of a doubt. Not one will go under or drown on the way after getting into Jesus' boat and holding fast to Him like a child. He is the Lord over heaven and earth. He has overcome and disarmed all life-threatening powers.

We should encourage one another when we see that storms are gathering; we should remind each other that Jesus is not absent, but that we are called to trust Him with our whole hearts in the midst of all our fears. This is true for the short stretches as well as for the long ones. As truly as Jesus does not go under, neither will we. The Lord who commands the wind and the waves can also change our situation from one moment to the next. He really can!

HOPE – ANCHOR OF THE SOUL

Now these three remain: faith, hope and love.

(1 Corinthians 13:13)

Day 57

WILL THERE STILL BE HOPE IN HEAVEN?

What is hope? Why do we need hope? How can we acquire hope? How do we nurture hope? What happens when there is no hope? I don't consider it time wasted to ponder the mystery, yes, the phenomenon of hope. Not only do we sense that a person who loses all hope has a poor chance of survival, God's Word also tells us that hope will accompany us in all eternity.

According to the great song of love in 1 Corinthians 13, one day all gifts and abilities will lose their meaning – all except love, faith and hope. These three, it says, will remain in all eternity. Therefore it is important to ask ourselves how we perceive hope, what it has to do with us and how real it is in our daily lives.

There is a negative proverb which says, "Hoping and persevering makes one a fool." The person who coined this saying had his own concept of hope. But what does this word "hope" really mean for us? Is it more than a pious concept or place of escape to which our soul flees for comfort when goals and desires are not fulfilled, so we're not overwhelmed by disappointment and pain? What do we associate with this term?

Too often the term "hope" is a bit hazy for us, so that we're rather surprised when Paul says that hope remains in all eternity. As someone rightly asked me, "If we're in heaven where we know and see everything, what is there to hope for? Why this hope in heaven?" Behind this question there is also a certain concept of hope. We often say of a person, "He's my last hope" when we want him to solve a problem we can't cope with. A person becomes the fulfillment of a concrete expectancy. This kind of thinking is quite biblical. In 1 Timothy 1:1 we read that Jesus Christ is our hope, meaning that Paul sees Jesus as the embodiment and fulfillment of our expectancy.

Hope obviously has to do with expectancy, which contains the word "expect." If we expect something we must wait for it. Thus hope has to do with waiting for something. Must we then wait for something in heaven? Apparently so, otherwise hope would hold no eternal dimension.

Day 58

WAITING FOR WHAT?

This, of course, begs the question of what it is that we must wait for in heaven. Generally we think of "waiting" as a rather unpleasant, often tense experience. We want to put it behind us as quickly as possible in order to attain what we are expecting. No one enjoys waiting. Most of us want to have the thing we are expecting immediately, painlessly and if possible without cost. The fact is that money and influence do bring countless opportunities to shorten or avoid waiting. But ultimately we must accept the fact that waiting is part of our humanity.

What actually happens when we are waiting? Does time simply slip past? Is precious time lost? Hardly, for in eternity time does not pass and there we must nevertheless wait. In nature, waiting is a growth process and growth means that fruit is ripening. Something also grows in us when we wait, especially when we wait expectantly. What grows depends directly on what we are waiting for or what we expect. Our attitude and sense of expectancy during the waiting process determine the fruit.

Life, longing, joy or peace do not grow automatically. We could also grow in frustration, anger or bitterness. This depends on what we hope and wait for; on what our heart is anticipating.

Day 59

DEAD HOPE AND LIVING HOPE

Let us return to the term "hope." In Romans 5:5 we read,

> Hope does not disappoint us, because God has poured out his love into our hearts by the Holy Spirit, whom he has given us.

The hope of which God's Word speaks does not disappoint, does not prove empty, but attains its goal and brings forth its fruit. The guarantee that this hope will not disappoint us is simply the fact that God has poured His love into our hearts. God's hope is thus based on, anchored in and directed through His love. Love is the source, substance and impetus of biblical hope. Hope depends on love!

We are not speaking of hope per se, for unfortunately there are many harmful types of hope. We need only look at history. Many revolutions which intended to create more justice and freedom began with hope and ended in frustration, in new forms of slavery, misery and death – all tasteless, inedible or even poisonous fruits. But it began with great hope for something new.

In 1 Peter 1:3 we read,

> Praise be to the God and Father of our Lord Jesus Christ! In his great mercy he has given us new birth into a living hope through the resurrection of Jesus Christ from the dead...

We have been born again to a living hope! So there are obviously dead hopes, as well, which are based not in the living God, but in man's dead spirit and in his unstable, unpredictable and unreliable soul. These dead hopes lead nowhere because their source and goal is not God Himself, but rather the man who is separated from and independent of God, the man who builds on himself.

God's Word is unmistakably clear regarding fruit born of man-based hope. Jeremiah says,

"Cursed is the one who trusts in man,
who depends on flesh [man's strength] for his strength [hope]
and whose heart turns away from the Lord.
He will be like a bush in the wastelands;
he will not see prosperity when it comes.
He will dwell in the parched places of the desert,
in a salt land where no-one lives."

(Jeremiah 17:5-6)

Day 60

BEING A LIVING HOPE

But the prophet also presents us with a picture of living hope,

> "But blessed is the man who trusts in the Lord,
> whose confidence is in him.
> He will be like a tree planted by the water
> that sends out its roots by the stream.
> It does not fear when heat comes;
> its leaves are always green.
> It has no worries in a year of drought
> and never fails to bear fruit."
>
> (Jeremiah 17:7-8)

If we place the guilt of our own ways under God's judgment on the cross and capitulate from our hearts, we experience salvation. Then God's love will be poured into our hearts for Jesus' sake. Jesus will become our hope. The roots of our being then receive access to living water which flows from God's heart. With this water we grow into a tree which produces life-creating fruit in all circumstances. We will not only have a living hope, we will also become a living hope for others because He who is hope lives in us.

Do we believe that we have a living – not an empty – hope and are we a hope for others if Jesus really lives in us? How tangible for others is the hope within us? Do people we encounter notice the water in which our roots are anchored? Can they taste the fruit which grows on our tree of life? If it is not clear to us what God's Word means by fruit, we can read in Paul's letter to the Galatians about "love, joy, peace, patience, kindness, goodness, faithfulness, gentleness and self-control" (see Galatians 5:22-23).

Day 61

HOPE MUST BE PROFESSED
AND FIRMLY GRASPED

Hope which is anchored in Jesus is a state of being and a visible profession of commitment. What is our orientation, what forms us, to whom or what do we expose ourselves, where do we belong? In Hebrews 10:23 we read,

> Let us hold unswervingly to the hope we profess, for he who promised is faithful.

Hope is a profession of what we are hoping for, to whom we belong, whom and what we are waiting for.

Hope is concrete. It includes tangible promises of an inheritance and a future, as written in 1 Corinthians 2:9,

> "No eye has seen, no ear has heard, no mind has conceived what God has prepared for those who love him…"

And in Romans 8:17-18,

> Now if we are children, then we are heirs – heirs of God and co-heirs with Christ, if indeed we share in his sufferings in order that we may also share in his glory. [For] I consider that

our present sufferings are not worth comparing with the glory that will be revealed in us.

We should cling to the substance and the foundation of our hope because the guarantor of this hope is absolutely reliable and faithful!

Clinging is an active act and attitude. In this world, the devil and his cronies attempt to steal whatever we do not consciously hold fast. The devil does not respect others' possessions, for he is a thief, a liar and a murderer. Therefore Jesus calls to us in Revelation 3:11,

> "I am coming soon. Hold on to what you have, so that no-one will take your crown."

So the substance of our hope, of what we may expect, is beyond the range and understanding of every human concept because it is anchored in God's heart. Only God can guarantee such a hope, for it is nothing less than transformation into Jesus' image, His being, His love and humility, His beauty and glory. For in 1 John 3:2-3 it is written,

> ...we shall be like him...Everyone who has this hope in him purifies himself, just as he is pure.

HOPE IS NOURISHED BY GOD'S WORD

Our hope must not only be declared and firmly held, but also purified and nourished. What nourishes my hope? In Romans 15:4 we read,

> everything...was written to teach us, so that through endurance and the encouragement of the Scriptures we might have hope.

So hope comes from endurance (holding fast) and from the encouragement of Scriptures, i.e. through confidence in God's promises.

Some Scripture passages indicate how God's Word builds hope, fills it with substance and directs it toward fulfillment. In 1 Timothy 4:10 Paul articulates the foundation of hope, "we have put our hope in the living God." In 1 Peter 1:13 God's Word calls to us, "be self-controlled; set your hope fully on the grace to be given you when Jesus Christ is revealed," and in 1 Timothy 1:1 Paul writes that Jesus Christ is our hope. Therefore we should set our hope exclusively on His grace. The prophet Jeremiah says to God, "For you are my hope" (Jeremiah 17:14, translated from the German Jerusalem Bible). If Jesus, who is the hope of glory, really lives in us, then we are living exhibits of hope. Therefore Peter's words make sense, "Always be prepared to give an answer to everyone who asks you to give the reason for the hope that you have" (1 Peter 3:15).

People who are searching for hope should be able to receive it from us – not because we know all the answers, but because the living God dwells in us with His promises! Because Jesus is the substance and goal of all hope, God's Word is also saturated with this theme. One could say that hope streams toward us from every page of the Bible.

We will now concentrate on the following verses:

> By two unchangeable things in which it is impossible for God to lie, we...may be greatly encouraged.
>
> (Hebrews 6:18)

The two unchangeable things are that God has given us His promises and that He has even confirmed them with an oath in His own name.

> [W]e who have fled to take hold of the hope offered to us may be greatly encouraged. We have this hope as an anchor for the soul, firm and secure. It enters the inner sanctuary behind the curtain...
>
> (Hebrews 6:18b-19)

When our soul is shaken by storms or drifts on the waves of this world's events, emotions, opinions and fears, this verse encourages us. It speaks of an anchor which we all need in order that we will not be driven off course or torn loose in such times.

Day 63

HOPE IS AN ANCHOR FOR OUR SOULS

What is the anchor for our souls? Hope. If our soul is torn loose by a storm and drifts helplessly, it does not require great intelligence to see that it was insecurely anchored. In other words, hope was lacking. In our daily lives hope is crucial: in our relationship with ourselves, with Jesus, with people around us; in regard to our commission, our calling and work. Our soul is anchored in this reality of hope.

Our hope is an anchor which is secured behind the curtain in the tent of meeting. That was the Most Holy Place, the place of God's presence, which only the high priest could enter once a year. In the tabernacle was also the throne of grace with the mercy seat, where God revealed Himself to His people.

Without going into further details regarding the tent of meeting, I want to emphasize one thought regarding hope. Behind the curtain, as I said, was the throne of grace – the place of forgiveness and daily new beginnings with myself and my neighbor. By God's mercy, no guilt is so great that it cannot be forgiven; no wound so great that it cannot be healed; no life so broken that it cannot be restored. Whoever turns daily to God's mercy in Jesus can know that,

If God is for us [and in Jesus, God is absolutely for us!], who can be against us? He who did not spare his own Son, but gave him up for us all – how will he not also, along with him, graciously give us all things?

(Romans 8:31-32)

Here "all things" means life, peace, freedom, joy and an indestructible future. When life's storms break over us with illness, problems, danger and finally death, we who have anchored our souls in God's throne of grace can say,

The Lord is my light and my salvation –
whom shall I fear?
The Lord is the stronghold of my life –
of whom shall I be afraid?

(Psalm 27:1)

If our souls are anchored behind the curtain, we will know God's care daily. He will say to us, "I know what thoughts I have about you, namely thoughts of salvation, to give a future to you and not only you, but to each one who turns to Me in trust. You have no reason for fear, resignation or discouragement. I am totally for you and will never abandon you until I have fulfilled everything I have promised."

God is absolutely reliable; in Him there is no falsehood. If we expose ourselves daily to this truth and fill our hearts, our minds and our wills with it, God's kingdom will become increasingly real and eternal fruits will ripen.

Day 64

HOPE AS THE BASIS OF FAITH

We said that hope is eternal because it has to do with Jesus Himself. It has to do with God's character. Hope is the reality which aligns us with God, knowing that God always has an answer to what we don't see or understand at the moment. Hope is the eternally open door in our lives. Hope is the reality that Jesus is the Yes and Amen to all God's promises in His Word (see 2 Corinthians 1:20). Every promise which was ever given must one day be fulfilled. Hope is the channel through which God's promises flow into our lives and the lives of others.

Some people may now ask what the difference is between hope and faith. Faith simply cannot exist without hope. Hebrews 11:1 explains the relationship between hope and faith.

> Now faith is being sure of what we hope for and certain of what we do not see.

Thus hope is a basis of faith. Whoever cannot hope cannot have faith, because he has nothing to cling to or expect. Where there is hope there is faith: faith makes our hope firm and permanent. No faith can exist without hope. If there is no hope, what then should we believe?

Day 65

I KNOW WHOM I BELIEVE IN

Hope is so central because it keeps our eyes fixed on God's promises for ourselves and for this world. In faith we can hold fast to the fact that God is good, God is here, God knows about my situation. If we bring this to Him and entrust ourselves to Him, He will act. God will come in His time, which is never too late! The works of the devil will be destroyed. Jesus will return soon and there will be no more pain, misery or need. This is no cheap comfort, but a hope which must be oriented by God's Word and clung to in faith!

Yes, many Moslems will find Jesus and enter God's kingdom! The people of Israel will recognize Jesus as their Messiah and King, thus completing God's joy. This is justified faith! Why? Because Jesus is the guarantor and He Himself is the hope. Therefore it is written,

> Let us hold unswervingly to the hope we profess, for he who promised is faithful.
>
> (Hebrews 10:23)

Holding on unswervingly means that we continually apply God's promises and remind God of them daily.

David is a model for us. Whenever for some reason he began losing his vision for his life or for a certain situation, he didn't throw in the towel, but turned to God and reminded Him of His promises.

Remember your word to your servant,
for you have given me hope.

(Psalm 119:49)

Lord, remember Your word! That is hope. Hope reminds God of His promises. It says to Him, "You are God and I am standing before You because You are everything for me. I'm waiting until You come, God. And You will come."

Here we see that hoping has much to do with persevering. Hope is the decisive heart attitude. It is the awareness and direction of our thoughts and wills; it is the awareness that God's kingdom will break through and be victorious. Of Jesus it is said,

"A bruised reed he will not break, and a smoldering wick he will not snuff out, till he leads justice to victory."

(Matthew 12:20)

Jesus is the guarantor. That is hope!

The question is whether we hold fast to it. If we have this hope for our lives, the devil can buffet us from left and right. What is anchored is anchored. Even if the waves are great, I can say with Paul, "I know whom I have believed" (2 Timothy 1:12).

Day 66

CALLED TO HOPE

Do we have hope and are we a real hope for others? Do we believe that God with His promises will achieve His purpose in our lives and in those around us? There is really only one hopeless case: the devil. But for God, no human is a hopeless case. Even when we reach the end of our tether, we must remain convinced that for God there is no hopeless case because hope has to do with His character. He himself is the hope. Therefore hope is eternal. And we will hope in all eternity because we are moving ever deeper into God's being. In all eternity we will know His salvation and His character more deeply.

Our hope is that we will be transformed into Jesus' image. This will never be completed! If the transformation of our hearts ended when we died, that would be insufficient for all of us. Thank God that He has greater goals for us. God is an eternal God and so we, too, will eternally grow into the character of His Son. That is my personal hope. Therefore I will invest and attempt everything in order to grow into Jesus' image on this earth. This is a very special time. But my hope is that the transformation will continue beyond my earthly life.

I repeat: our soul's anchor is our hope regarding God's promises for us, our friends, our congregations and families. People with much hope are people with a big heart and a broad horizon. People with hope expect much from God. One cannot have hope and yet remain narrow-minded or lack joy and peace.

I want to encourage all of us to expose ourselves to this reality of hope and cling to the profession of hope. For we know: hope does not disappoint us because it has to do with God's character and the basis of this hope is God's love.

Section 8

THE WAITING FATHER

"There was a man who had two sons. The younger one said to his father, 'Father, give me my share of the estate.' So he divided his property between them. Not long after that, the younger son got together all he had, set off for a distant country and there squandered his wealth in wild living. After he had spent everything, there was a severe famine in that whole country, and he began to be in need. So he went and hired himself out to a citizen of that country, who sent him to his fields to feed pigs. He longed to fill his stomach with the pods that the pigs were eating, but no-one gave him anything. When he came to his senses, he said, 'How many of my father's hired men have food to spare, and here I am starving to death! I will set out and go back to my father and say to him: Father, I have sinned against heaven and against you. I am no longer worthy to be called your son; make me like one of your hired men.' So he got up and went to his father. But while he was still a long way off, his father saw him and was filled with compassion for him; he ran to his son, threw his arms around him and kissed him. The son said to him, 'Father, I have sinned against heaven and against you. I

am no longer worthy to be called your son.' But
the father said to his servants, 'Quick! Bring the
best robe and put it on him. Put a ring on his
finger and sandals on his feet. Bring the fattened
calf and kill it. Let's have a feast and celebrate.
For this son of mine was dead and is alive again;
he was lost and is found.' So they began
to celebrate."

(Luke 15:11-24)

Day 67

THE WAITING FATHER

Father – what do we associate with this term, this title, this status? Trust, protection, strength and longing for security, acceptance, belonging. But perhaps also pain, disappointment, anger and bitterness.

Fatherhood is a mystery we must continually rediscover because it pertains to all of us existentially. It is so existential that Jesus made God's fatherhood the starting point for all true prayer when we come before God. "This, then, is how you should pray: 'Our Father in heaven...'" (Matthew 6:9). Without grasping and experiencing God's fatherhood, we will never find ourselves or inner peace. Therefore we can never strive enough for God's Spirit to reveal to us what it means that God is our Father.

We know the story of the prodigal son only too well. It is one of the stories we have all heard many times, from Sunday school to confirmation class, then role-played in youth groups, quite apart from all the sermons. It really is a very pivotal story! But it is usually told from the younger son's point of view. We are struck by his rebellion, his downfall, his pitiful situation in the pigsty and his remorse. And this certainly is moving! Nevertheless, I don't want to call this story "The Prodigal Son," but "The Waiting Father."

Normally we consider the son the central figure, both when he left home and when he returned. We understand the celebration at the end of the story as primarily a party for the son who returned...

Day 68

THE FATHER'S HUMILIATION

However, I believe that Jesus told this story not just because of the son, but to say something about the father. For Jesus, the father was the central figure. He came to reveal the Father and to show His contemporaries: See what a Father God is!

It was easy for everyone to identify with the story of the son, with a young person who chose such a path. Wherever they looked, this was a reality. This was nothing new for any father who was standing there. They were familiar with rebellion, opposition and disappointment over their sons. Many of them had such a son themselves or they knew of the neighbor's son. The novel thing was what Jesus said about the father. Here we see a father who first of all lets himself be humiliated. He was willing to be demeaned, wounded and derided. But in order to truly understand the depth of the father's humiliation we must consider its cultural context.

At that time, dividing the inheritance was an official matter. Such a thing wasn't done secretly! This son had taken the inheritance and left, which made the rift between father and son public. Everyone could see that the father had been deserted and dishonored by his own son. And no oriental father would put up with this. To the people listening his behavior was an outrage. So their attention was caught from the opening of the story. They probably asked themselves, "How is such a thing possible? No father would let himself be humiliated like the one in Jesus' story." I think they were all eager to hear how this father would react. How would this continue? A father who let himself be hurt! Why does he behave like this?

Day 69

THE VULNERABLE GOD

At first, the answer is obvious for all of us who are Bible-trained. This father allows himself to be hurt and humiliated because love is his nature and his very being. There is no other reason for him to put up with this. In this world, expressed love is unavoidably interwoven with suffering. Without exaggerating we can say that, in this world, to love is to suffer. For we read, "darkness covers the earth and thick darkness is over the peoples" (Isaiah 60:2) and "the thoughts of his [man's] heart were only evil all the time" (Genesis 6:5). Jesus came to seek, to love and to save the lost, the strays and the guilt-afflicted. Love for us who are lost and laden with guilt brought Him inconceivable suffering and finally death.

Because God is love, the possibility of suffering existed even before man's fall and I believe that God suffered. He was wounded and humiliated by His own creation, for example in the rebellion of one of His most senior angels, Lucifer. It must have hurt God to see that someone could so misinterpret His nature, His thoughts and His goals for creation that he thought he could find more fulfillment outside a relationship with God. It is an absolutely tragic, but also deadly misunderstanding to think that rebelling against God can bring more than obeying Him.

Turning away from God is ultimately always pride, and there is nothing which wounds more than pride and arrogance. Arrogance is the belief that we can make more of our lives on our own than God intended for us. The arrogance of putting our own view of life above God's word hurts Him deeply.

Day 70

GOD FORCES NO ONE

If God had wanted to be invulnerable He would have had to remove from creation the possibility of saying "No" to Him, the creator; and that He did not do. God is love, and no one can be compelled to love. Not even God can do that! The possibility of saying "No" always includes the possibility that love will suffer. That is what happened to God. In the story of the waiting father, Jesus wants to tell us, "Look, because the Father is love, He is abased and lets Himself be wounded." It is in the nature of genuine love that, if it seeks and loves the other for his own sake, this will mean suffering. This is true of love between man and woman, between parents and children, and between friends. It is true of every sort of love in this world and especially of God's love for us.

Wherever we find misunderstanding and arrogance in a relationship, love will suffer. It means that one person in the relationship is focused on himself, that he is using and misusing the other party merely as a source of "raw material" to build himself up. This brings suffering with it. In this world there is no way to express love without going through and accepting such suffering. For we live in a fallen creation with persons whose hearts need salvation and healing.

It is important for us to understand that in God's relationship with us He is not simply above everything. He really suffers because He loves. He suffers because of our narrow hearts, our mendacity, our cowardice, our pride, our egoism and our greed for life. We tend to turn away quickly the minute we are hurt or disappointed. But God suffers because He does not dissociate Himself from us; He bears the misunderstanding. If He turned away, He would not have to suffer.

Day 71

HE LOVED THEM TO THE END

We will look at some verses in the Gospel of John, where we read,

> It was just before the Passover Feast. Jesus knew that the time had come for him to leave this world and go to the Father. Having loved his own who were in the world, he now showed them the full extent of his love [German: loved them to the end (Jerusalemer Bibel)]. The evening meal was being served, and the devil had already prompted Judas Iscariot, son of Simon, to betray Jesus. Jesus knew that the Father had put all things under his power, and that he had come from God and was returning to God; so he got up from the meal, took off his outer clothing, and wrapped a towel around his waist. After that, he poured water into a basin and began to wash his disciples' feet, drying them with the towel that was wrapped round him.
>
> (John 13:1-5)

What does the expression "he loved them to the end" mean? Jesus knew His disciples and what they were capable of. He knew that Peter would deny Him. He knew that when He would most need His disciples' support – during His struggle in Gethsemane and on the cross – all but one would desert Him in order to save their own skins. He knew that all those sitting beside Him – with whom He had shared His life, to whom He had opened His heart wide to show them the Father – would end as cowards and traitors. Jesus had no illusions about His disciples, just as the father in our story had no illusions about a son who publicly humiliated and left him.

When it says, "he loved them to the end" it means that in full knowledge of their hearts and of what was coming, He did not cut Himself off from them. Because God is love He hates evil, sin and pride. But He does not turn from weakness, need and misery. Until the last moment, as long as there is still a spark of hope, He will stand by us. It is not by coincidence that it is written of Jesus,

> "A bruised reed he will not break,
> and a smoldering wick he will not snuff out.
> In faithfulness he will bring forth [God's] justice..."
>
> (Isaiah 42:3)

This is good news for us. Until the end, the Father will not turn from us, no matter what may come to the light. God knows about it and because He is love, He is willing to put up with everything until we begin to change. For in 1 Corinthians 13:7 we read that love always protects, always believes (even when we no longer believe), always hopes, always perseveres. This sort of love goes to the utmost!

Day 72

THE EVIL EYE

In the story of the prodigal son, Jesus described our heavenly Father, who is this love. This Father loves to the end, is not embittered over our pride, our arrogance or our faithlessness. He keeps on watching for us daily and does not tire of waiting for our return. With grief and shame He holds the door open for our return home. Mocked and scorned, wrongly deemed powerless, disdained as a stupid or even harmful projection of human fantasy, He waits outside the barricaded human hearts, outside the gates of the world until we leave our pigsties to return to Him. He takes us in His arms joyfully, in spite of all our stench and filth. Do we who call ourselves His sons and daughters go out to bear His disgrace with Him (see Hebrews 13:13)? Or are we like the older son who abandons the father to wait alone, the son who is unable to share his father's joy over the younger son's return?

How much the father must have suffered here, as well, and how much the older son misjudges his father! He must recite his own needs and merits and struggle for his place and his rights. A flood of accusations and resentment, revealing massive alienation from the father's heart, is poured on the father. The older sons and daughters, who may include us, are quick to calculate and to demand their rights. Because, tragically, we often serve for rewards, we

171

can hardly bear the encounter with God's goodness which alone can lead to repentance and return. This extravagant goodness, which receives the last arrival with the same generosity as the first, becomes a stumbling block ("an evil eye," as God's Word says in Matthew 6:23 or Luke 11:34 KJV) insofar as the Father's love has not yet taken control of our heart.

In the parable of the laborers in the vineyard (Matthew 20:1-16) Jesus makes us painfully aware of this. As long as we have not allowed Jesus to lead us to the Father's heart, we will know the Father only by hearsay. We will view the world, the brother or the sister with an "evil eye" which encounters all the good and all the blessing in others' lives with envy, resentment and mistrust. We will be quick to suppose that God and those He has blessed have acted from impure motives. In this case the Father cannot share His joy with us, no matter how much He longs to. The Father's love seeks to liberate us from our evil eye so that He can flood us with His joy.

Day 73

FOR THEY DO NOT
KNOW WHAT THEY DO

Now back to our story. The father lets his son leave – in silence! We are reminded of Luke 23:34, where Jesus prays for those who will crucify Him, "Father, forgive them, for they do not know what they are doing." At first this seems as if He is excusing them, but He is not. It is no light matter when we do not know what we're doing. To say that people don't know what they are doing means they cannot be taken seriously. Those who don't know what they're doing are either very small children or seriously handicapped people who cannot carry responsibility.

The statement "for they do not know what they are doing" causes the Father deep pain. Why? Because they could have known. Those who crucified Jesus, or the son who left the father, could all have known who the Father is because He reveals Himself to them every day through His care, His goodness and His love. In Romans 1:20 we read,

> For since the creation of the world God's invisible qualities – his eternal power and divine nature – have been clearly seen, being understood from what has been made, so that men are without excuse.

Arrogance and pride so darken our senses that we are incapable of perceiving God. Our hearts are hardened until they become numb and loveless stones. But even then love does not give up. Because Jesus knows the Father's heart, He prays, "Father, forgive them!" He knows that the Father is able to turn hearts of stone into hearts of flesh. The Father does not give up even though by waiting He makes Himself a laughing-stock to everyone, even to all of creation. He tolerates it when others say, "How can You keep on waiting for such a person! Look how utterly rotten this son is. He dishonors and wounds You in front of everyone. He squanders Your fortune without conscience!"

I think it very probable that the angels are often deeply ashamed of the way we treat the Father; that they who know what He is really like are amazed that He puts up with such disgraceful behavior. But in fact this Father does put up with it!

Day 74

REPENTANCE THROUGH GOD'S GOODNESS

Then repentance comes. The son's repentance is the fruit of the waiting father's suffering. It was God's goodness and mercy which not only kept the son alive but finally led him to repent. Then the son is received in his father's house. If we are sons and daughters of this Father, if we are close to His heart, our goodness will make it possible for others to repent of broken relationships. Then we can communicate to them that after a broken relationship – whether a friendship, a marriage, or parent-child and other family relationships – there is a way back home.

The person who demonstrates and offers such a message of goodness and forgiveness will suffer. But it will facilitate restoration and healing; it will create lasting fruit which honors the Father. If we reach the end of our rope and don't know where to turn, then we may know that we can return any time! No matter what happens, we can return! The Father permitted Himself to become a laughing-stock in just this way. He let his rightful honor be trampled underfoot in order to keep the door open for this son. That is grace. Paul wrote, "Do you not realize that God's goodness leads you to repentance?" (cf. Romans 2:4). Through everything this goodness reminds us that we have a home!

Day 75

ENTRUSTING OURSELVES TO GOD

When this goodness reached its goal and the son – who had outwardly and inwardly landed in the gutter – finally set out to return to his father, his first thoughts were of remorse and repentance. "I'm no longer worthy to be called your son!" That is correct, for we are all unworthy to be called His sons and daughters. But this repentance and contrition do not last long. Soon the son began giving his father advice: "Make me one of your servants!" Hardly have we taken the first step back to the Father's house than we begin imagining how God should treat us. That all sounds so humble, but deep down it is pride. We judge ourselves a bit in order to demonstrate that we really aren't so bad and still know our place. We are familiar with this attitude. It often comes in the form of self-accusation and self-judgment, dictating to God what He should think of us – instead of wholly entrusting ourselves to this Father and simply praying, "Lord, be merciful to me, a sinner!"

God knows how to treat us without our advice. It is enough simply to listen to Him and say,

My father,
I give myself to you,
Do whatever you want with me.
Whatever you want to do with me, I thank you.
I am ready for everything, I accept everything.
If only your will is fulfilled in me
And in all your creatures,
Then I long for nothing further, my God.
I lay my soul in your hands;
I give it to you, my God
With all the love of my heart, because I love you
And because this love drives me
To give myself to you,
To lay myself in your hands,
Without measure, with unlimited trust.
For you are my father!

(Charles de Foucauld)

That is unconditional repentance. Because Paul had grasped that, he wrote, "I care very little about what others say about me. I do not even judge myself" (see 1 Corinthians 4:3). He knew that self-judgment is meaningless and proud. God is the only one who judges us. He is the one who carries out the judgment – not we ourselves. Thank God for that!

The story of the prodigal son demonstrates how the heavenly Father handles this. "While he was still a long way off, his father saw him and was filled with compassion for him; he ran to his son, threw his arms around him and kissed him." Before the son could say a word he experienced the father's mercy and love. This father was not too proud to express his joy, even to abandon himself to it, and throw his arms around his son. At least at this moment we might have expected the father to show a bit of dignity and to wait for a small apologetic gesture from his son, so that everyone could see that he had some self-respect. Nothing like it! He even ran toward his son as soon as he saw him. In the culture of that time, it was totally inappropriate – especially for an authority figure such as a father – to show emotions in this way. But out of love this father put aside all reservation and dignity in order to express unmistakably, "You are expected! I have waited for you!"

Day 76

RETURNING HOME

There is an impressive story from China about a certain son who likewise wanted to return home. It is a good illustration for our story of the prodigal son. A son leaves his father and goes to the city in order to earn money. The father, who really needs him at home on the farm, is left back alone and sad. The son knows that this bruises the relationship with his father, but won't give up his plans. He spends a few unsuccessful years in the city, finally ending up in the gutter. His dream of a proud return is shattered. He decides to return to his father, but – remembering all too well how he had left – is full of scruples. So he writes to his father that he would return home by train and if his father wanted him back, he should hang a white cloth in a certain tree in the garden.

As the train enters his village, he asks the man sitting next to him to look out the window to see whether there is a white cloth hanging from a certain tree. He closes his eyes and waits. Finally his fellow traveler answers that he can't see a tree with one white cloth on it, but there is a tree totally covered with white cloths. The father had obviously been waiting impatiently for his son!

Matthew 7:11 tells us,

"If you, then, though you are evil, know how to give good gifts to your children, how much more will your Father in heaven give good gifts to those who ask him!"

Let me paraphrase this verse thus: "If you, then, though you are evil, can wait for your children, how much more will your Father in heaven wait for His children!"

At the end of the story of the prodigal son, the father said, "Let's have a feast and celebrate!" After the father had embraced him, the son repented, after all. And while he was still repenting, the father proceeded to the next point, the celebration. Repentance always restores relationships, leading to joy and celebration. The son is not the center of this celebration. It is the father's party because he is so happy that his love, which reached out to the uttermost, ultimately brought his son back to life. He cries out, "For this son of mine was dead and is alive again."

This love which continues to the end will raise people from the dead. It will create life such as Jesus had. Jesus Himself loved His disciples until the end. He loved Peter, the one who denied Him, so much that Peter later became an apostle. This is ultimately a resurrection from the dead, the creation of new life. And all of this takes place through the love which perseveres! What good news that we have such a Father!

Section 9

JESUS' RETURN

"See, I will send my messenger, who will prepare
the way before me. Then suddenly the Lord you
are seeking will come to his temple; the messenger of the covenant, whom you desire, will
come," says the Lord Almighty. "But who can
endure the day of his coming? Who can stand
when he appears? For he will be like a refiner's
fire or a launderer's soap. He will sit as a refiner
and purifier of silver; he will purify the Levites
and refine them like gold and silver. Then the
Lord will have men who will bring offerings
in righteousness..."

(Malachi 3:1-3)

Day 77

LONGING FOR HOME

We celebrate Advent every year. It is therefore not only meaningful, but almost necessary that we take it as an opportunity to ask ourselves just what sort of an arrival – for "Advent" means "arrival" – we are really expecting, if indeed we expect anything at all. I realize that in general Advent is considered a time of preparation for Christmas. But unfortunately we're usually so busy with all the preparations that the resulting stress even threatens our health. There are more than a few of us who, chased by dates, duties and expectations, have only one wish: to get this time behind us as quickly as possible.

This may seem a bit over-dramatic. But Advent is in fact a dramatic time because our hustle and bustle is not the sole source of stress. In the Christian and Christianized world there is no other time of the year when people's emotions are so churned up. Longings and desires overwhelm us. Many are concerned, even if subconsciously, with questions about belonging, home and family. Loneliness and homelessness can seem a crushing void, an abyss of being lost. The massive increase in depressive illnesses during this season speaks a clear message.

These are not empty clichés. On the contrary, in our culture there is hardly anything sadder than someone who has no place of fellowship, belonging, acceptance or security on Christmas Eve. The longing for a home and security is an existential need. Not by coincidence is it so overpowering during this season, for the mystery is that we celebrate the birth and arrival of the one who came to lead us out of the abyss of homelessness, lostness and darkness – back to our eternal home.

In the Bible we read that Jesus came to seek and save the lost. He came to lead us out of darkness into light, out of bondage into freedom, out of death into life. He will bring each one who entrusts himself to Him, who puts his life into His hands, to the place of which we read, "Now the dwelling of God is with men!...There will be no more death or mourning or crying or pain..." (Revelation 21:3-4). This describes the final home-coming. Who does not long for this! It sounds like a utopian, unrealistic dream. But God, who knows our lack of faith and imagination, reassures us precisely, "these words are trustworthy and true!" (Revelation 21:5).

Day 78

THE GREATEST EVENT
THE WORLD HAS EVER SEEN

Whoever comes through the narrow gate of faith to Jesus' cross experiences God's life breaking powerfully into this world's valley of death. "The light shines in the darkness" (John 1:5). Jesus' cross became the heavenly ladder by which God descended to men in order to lead them home to Himself. There Jesus opened the door wide and He is still challenging us to set out for that place.

Jesus Himself returned to the Father with a very concrete goal. In John 14:2-3 He said that He would prepare a home for us with the Father and would then return to fetch us so that we could always be where He is. Paul, who through grace was allowed to look into heaven, said of this home, "No eye has seen, no ear has heard...what God has prepared for those who love him" (1 Corinthians 2:9). The beauty, security, peace and joy of this home with God surpasses all human power of imagination.

Is this an unrealistic utopia, a desperate projection of our longings and desires? No, not if we believe God's Word. If we believe Jesus' promises (and it is in our best interests to do so!), we can wait confidently for this promise's fulfillment.

For we read of God,

"God is not a man, that he should lie, nor a son of man, that he should change his mind. Does he speak and then not act? Does he promise and not fulfill?"

(Numbers 23:19)

This is not a matter of empty promises for the coming world, but of the question: How do we regard the coming event that will prove to be the greatest the world has ever seen? Namely that Jesus, the Messiah and Son of God, to whom the Father had subjected all things (see John 13:3), will return to get His Bride, the Church; that He is coming to clarify once and for all the question of His reign over His people Israel and over all people! Do we believe that this will take place as promised? Do we expect Jesus to return as the judge of the old creation (see John 5:22-24) and as Lord of the new one? If so, what is our attitude as we expect Him?

Day 79

GOD FULFILLS HIS WORD

We must ask ourselves this question especially during Advent, the season in which we consciously await Jesus' return. In many places it is a tradition to light an additional candle every Sunday during Advent. Light is a symbol of God's presence, of hope, peace and joy. Therefore Jesus said, "I am the light of the world" (John 8:12). By lighting an Advent candle we testify that we hope and wait for the return of the Messiah Jesus; we hope for the complete restoration of all things and the simultaneous dawn of God's eternal kingdom.

When we lose our vision and our joyful hope through circumstances, shocks, short-sightedness or lethargy, we must determinedly get up again and return to God's promises. Then He can renew and strengthen our vision, our hope and our joyful expectancy of what is coming. For if we lose sight of God's coming kingdom, we will easily lose sight of His present kingdom, as well.

"if I go and prepare a place for you, I will come back and take you to be with me that you also may be where I am."

(John 14:3)

Of course, someone might say, "Well, we can't really take this story about Jesus' return so literally." I know many people who interpret it figuratively. For all those who are not quite certain or who find it hard to believe that Jesus will return, I want to assure you that it will be similar to the founding of the nation of Israel. In spite of all human reason and calculation, in spite of world resistance throughout millennia and into our time, God has fulfilled the promises He gave to the Jewish people thousands of years ago. Who would have thought, seventy or eighty years ago, that very soon everyone would speak about a nation of Israel, as we do today?

God promised to gather His people and make them a nation again. And He did it! One can resist this fact; one can dislike the Jewish people or entertain many questions about their behavior – but the nation exists because God promised its restoration. And just as God fulfilled His word regarding Israel's restoration, so He will also fulfill His word regarding Jesus' return. God does not use empty words. We can rest assured of that.

Day 80

THE MESSIAH'S TWO SIDES

If God promised us something, then He really means it, just as He said. The verses from Malachi 3:1-3 regarding the Messiah's coming are a message to the Jewish people. But they are likewise a message to the body of Christ. I will not deal with the message to the Jewish people as a nation, but only with what I believe God says to His Church. This Church consists of Jews and non-Jews, of all the people in the whole world who believe in Jesus. Peter said of them, "you are a chosen people, a royal priesthood, a holy nation, a people belonging to God" (1 Peter 2:9).

In Revelation 19:7-8 this royal priesthood is also called the bride of Christ. Why is the Church called a bride? The terms "bride" and "bridegroom" express a very intimate relationship of the heart. The message is for the bride who is waiting for the bridegroom. What could a truly loving bride, who has given her heart to her bridegroom, desire more than being endlessly together with the one she loves?

We may perhaps say that we are surely looking forward to the coming of Jesus, the Messiah. For His coming is the fulfillment of all our longing; it is the end of all suffering, all need and all darkness in this world. Who does not yearn for this end?

But God's Word says that when the Messiah comes He will bring not only the end, but also the new beginning, whether we believe that or not. Yes, He comes to complete. Many Christians rejoice over this thought, and that is good. But now, if we look closely, our text in Malachi asks a question which is rather unsettling. We read, "who can endure the day of his coming?" This doesn't fit our picture of Jesus: the good shepherd, the savior to whom everyone can always come, with whom one surely finds acceptance. Then what does this mean? The Messiah really is both the good shepherd and the consuming fire!

Day 81

THE MESSIAH IS MERCIFUL

We are more familiar with the side described in Isaiah 42. The Messiah is the one who will not snuff out a smoldering wick and will not break a bruised reed (cf. v. 3). Because He is mercy itself He does not judge men's weakness. He is the one who turns to each person without demanding any advance achievement. He came to seek the lost. He is familiar with our need, with our struggle for life, with our suffering over ourselves. He knows us and has absolutely no illusions about us. He is familiar with the human heart's make-up and character. He sees through our facade. Thanks be to God that we cannot and must not pretend anything!

And He says, "I am the door" (John 10:9 KJV). Whoever comes to Jesus can be certain that He will take him home and lead him to life. He is our sole true hope because He alone is able to make us free and take us out of all our fears and everything which holds us captive, everything which restricts us and slowly but surely destroys us: bitterness, accusation, self-condemnation. Jesus knows that we are incapable of relationships either with ourselves or with others – our marriage partners, our children or our neighbors. He knows all that and doesn't shrink back because He is the Messiah, the savior of the world! Therefore He says to us, "You can come to Me, no matter how broken and bruised you are. I will make you whole, I will create something new in your life." This is good news!

WHO CAN STAND WHEN HE APPEARS?

Then there is the other side of the Messiah, of which prophet Malachi spoke. "Who can stand when he appears?" Obviously, the second coming of the Messiah will not be hidden and quiet like the first, but will be like the description in Matthew 24:27,

> "For as lightning that comes from the east is visible even in the west, will be the coming of the Son of Man."

Then the light will break into the darkness and thus into men's lives, ruling and demanding that men give account; it will unveil and expose to men God's reality and truth. What the Messiah's light reveals will be so shockingly unbearable that this world's powerful and proud will call to the mountains and rocks,

> "Fall on us and hide us from the face of him who sits on the throne and from the wrath of the Lamb! For the great day of their wrath has come, and who can stand?"
>
> (Revelation 6:16-17)

Today it is still possible to brag in God's presence. We can still develop many private theories about God and act as if our personal opinion and interpretation of our lives and world events mean just as much, if not more, than God's word. But when the Messiah comes all arguments will cease. We will simply be at a loss for words. In the presence of Him who is the truth and the light every lie will be silenced and all pride will collapse. Everything will be exposed and reduced to its own true essence. When He comes, our lives will be revealed. There will be nothing more to hide.

Man in his pride and his self-righteousness, in his self-made faith, in his arrogance and pride will have to enter the Messiah Jesus' presence. But in the darkness of his heart he will not be able to bear the countenance of Him who is the light. And yet it would be so easy before that day dawns for all men to avoid the coming judgment! In the present time of grace Jesus is struggling with all His means to forgive us and draw us into His light; so that when He comes we will be able to stand in His presence. What is demanded of us is really not much: to turn around, place our lives in His light, and let ourselves be helped out of pride, lies, guilt, self-righteousness and need. But it will cost us everything to humble ourselves in this way!

Day 83

WHO CAN BEAR HIS PRESENCE?

Because Jesus loves us He wants so much for us to be able to bear His presence when He comes. For He takes no pleasure in the death of the godless. In what condition will we come before Him? What sort of bride will we be? Will we be a bride whose heart is totally directed to Him, a heart longing for Him to return? Or will we be a bride who, although she knows that the bridegroom will come one day, is so taken up with herself that she has no time to think about how she will appear before Him?

When Jesus comes, His light will reveal what is inside us, even the most secret thoughts which we have been able to hide from others, who cannot see into our hearts. Let us not forget that God is always present! He is not pointing an accusing finger, but longing for our heart to be a place where He can reside. Truth, forgiveness and mercy should be found there, so that others see in us that God is a good God.

When He comes, He will cleanse us from our self-centeredness, our conceit and our pride; He will cleanse us from our narrow-mindedness, which so quickly and thoughtlessly judges other believers whose relationship to Jesus is not like ours. It is difficult to believe the extent to which our heart is penetrated by these disease-causing, destructive habits such as status seeking, envy, jealousy, miserliness, self-righteousness and dishonesty. Not even our prayers or our service for God are free of them. How often are we ourselves the real goal and the center of what we think and do!

Day 84

THE FIRE OF CLEANSING

When Jesus cleanses His bride it will be extremely painful. Not because He wants to punish us, no, but because without His grace we would not be able to bear the shame over our heart condition which His light reveals! Then we will realize that the way we have lived was a denial of His name. We will realize that we, His bride, have prostituted ourselves most of the time by giving our hearts to other lovers and lords – be it mammon and everything it offers; be it our religious self-righteousness which forbade fellowship with other Christians (who also set their hope in the cross of Christ), thus trampling underfoot our bridegroom's legacy and heart's desire; or be it our effort not to appear before the world as narrow-minded, fundamentalist and stubborn. All the time we have kept a noble distance from the claim of God's Word on our lives; we considered it out-dated and not binding, so that we wouldn't seem outsiders who lose the world's warmth and affection. How great must be the pain when we have the extent of the faithlessness, weakness and lack of character in our hearts before our eyes!

In 1 Corinthians 3:12-15, as in Malachi 3:2, we read of the fire which will test the substance of the works of God's people, the bride of Christ. It will be the fire of God's holiness which leaves in us only the eternal fruit of our likeness to Jesus. The only things in our hearts which will survive this fire are the aspects of Jesus' character which became reality. Our calling is to be changed into His likeness. This is what God made us for!

God will seek His Son's likeness in us. Jesus clearly stated the sign by which others could recognize that we are His disciples,

> "By this all men will know that you are my disciples, if you love one another."
>
> (John 13:35)

Not only the earth, but also the heavens will look for this sign.

ONLY OUR MOTIVES COUNT

We will be judged according to our love – our readiness to forgive and the mercy, kindness and purity of our motives. God is not impressed by our achievements because He is the one who gives us our power as well as our gifts or abilities. The motivation for our actions will be decisive, quite apart from our life's circumstances, our gifts and abilities, or what sort of work, position or responsibility we had.

A housewife whose fear of God and love for Jesus motivates her to invest her life in her children, her husband and the people who go in and out of her house has just as much chance to rise from the fire with riches and glory as people with many gifts who achieve great things in God's kingdom. God looks at our hearts. He will not be fooled.

Jesus clearly said,

> "If you obey my commands, you will remain in my love...My command is this: Love each other as I have loved you."
>
> (John 15:10, 12)

Our love must be real. When Jesus returns He could well ask us, "How do you treat your wife, your husband, your children, your work colleagues? Can it be seen that you belong to Me and that you love Me? Are you a person who builds others up through his daily behavior? One who encourages others to hope? One who does not attempt to use others to promote his ministry, his career or his life? Do you treat others in a way which encourages them to love Me, trust Me and follow Me? What are your priorities? What is important and central in your life? Where do you invest your energy, your power, your gifts, your possessions? Do you love Me?"

Revelation 2 gives us a very serious warning. It is a passionate call of the Messiah to the church in Ephesus. This church was in many ways exemplary – in its attitude under persecution and pressure and with its gift of discernment which retained pure and true doctrine, enabling it to differentiate between lies and truth. These people had probably established wide-ranging services to the poor, as well as much social work. But it seems that in all their activities for God they had increasingly lost sight of Him. He had to say to them,

> "Yet I hold this against you: You have forsaken your first love. Remember the height from which you have fallen! Repent and do the things you did at first. If you do not repent, I will come to you and remove your lampstand from its place."
>
> (Revelation 2:4-5)

God always desires a heart relationship, or as David put it in Psalm 51, "truth in the innermost parts" (v. 6, translated from the SLT German Bible).

PASSIONATELY EXPECTING JESUS

When the Messiah comes He will look for a bride who is expecting Him and has made herself beautiful for Him. How can a bride make herself beautiful for her bridegroom? In the Bible there is a mirror which Christ's bride can use to evaluate her beauty and her similarity to the Messiah Jesus. This mirror is found in Galatians 5:22-25. It describes how God's Spirit works on and prepares a heart which pleases God and makes it beautiful like a bride for her bridegroom:

> the fruit of the Spirit is love, joy, peace, patience, kindness, goodness, faithfulness, gentleness and self-control.
>
> (Galatians 5:22-23a)

May God help us be a bride who makes herself beautiful for her bridegroom every day, who passionately awaits His return, who calls to Him daily, "Come, Lord Jesus!", who runs toward Him joyfully. "The Spirit and the bride say, 'Come!' And let him who hears say, 'Come!'" (Revelation 22:17). And He is coming. As surely as the Lord, the God of Israel, is the living God!

Let us pray:

Holy Father, we are so grateful that Your Word is so clear; that You are a God who thoroughly knows us – His creatures, His children. No thought of ours is unknown to You. No word is on our tongues which You aren't familiar with. You want to help us come into Your light, into the truth about ourselves and about You. We are so grateful that You are the one who will prepare our hearts to receive the Messiah Jesus.

We ask You from our whole hearts, Holy Father, to help us become genuine in our relationship to You and to other people. Help us become people of the truth so that we can stand in your light and so that others can see in us hope and mercy, in which they can see and honor You. We ask You for Your good Holy Spirit to support us, to help us and to remove us from all our illusions about ourselves, from over-estimating ourselves, from dullness and lethargy. Holy Father, we ask You in the name of Your Messiah Jesus to be merciful to us. Amen.

Section 10

MY BROTHERS' KEEPER

If you have any encouragement from being
united with Christ, if any comfort from his love,
if any fellowship with the Spirit, if any tenderness
and compassion, then make my joy complete by
being like-minded, having the same love, being
one in spirit and purpose. Do nothing out of
selfish ambition or vain conceit, but in humility
consider others better than yourselves. Each of
you should look not only to your own interests,
but also to the interests of others. Your attitude
should be the same as that of Christ Jesus…

(Philippians 2:1-5)

Day 87

WHERE IS YOUR BROTHER?

Paul's words could be summarized in the question God asked Cain, "Where is your brother?" (Genesis 4:9). Or to put it another way, "What do you have to say about your brother? What is your relationship to him?" The question prompting this is really, "What is your relationship to Me? Who do you say I am?" For what erupted from Cain and caused him to murder his brother Abel was fundamentally his rage against God.

It is an eternal principle that our relationships to one another always reflect our relationship to God. Our relationships are a mirror of the reality of God's kingdom in our lives and of the way in which we know Him. The picture of Him which we carry in our hearts will always influence the way we relate to our neighbor. Or, in reverse, the way we relate to our neighbor reveals our relationship to God.

This cannot be otherwise. For God's essence is love. He created man in His own image, i.e. as a being capable of love. But love is expressed in our relationship to and our care for our neighbor. Therefore the epitome of everything which makes man's heart pleasing to God is encapsulated in the twin command of love.

Jesus replied, "'Love the Lord your God with all your heart and with all your soul and with all your mind.' This is the first and greatest commandment. And the second is like it: 'Love your neighbor as yourself.' All the law and the prophets hang on these two commandments."

(Matthew 22:37-40)

Day 88

THE GENUINENESS OF
OUR LOVE FOR JESUS

If we love God, if we belong to Him through Jesus and thus share His being, God's character will be visible to our neighbor through us. It is written of God that He loved the world so much that He gave what was most precious to Him, namely His Son, for the people of the world (see John 3:16). In Romans we read that He loved us while we were still His enemies. His love and care are beyond sympathy and antipathy. Through Jesus' cross God calls to those who since the Fall – contaminated in body, soul and spirit through disobedience and pride – are wandering in the dark, mortally ill and homeless, "I have plans to give you hope and a future" (cf. Jeremiah 29:11). "Seek me and live" (Amos 5:4). God wants to save, heal, cleanse and lead us from darkness into His light so that we will have a home with Him. Therefore we read, "If we walk in the light, as he is in the light, we have fellowship with one another" (1 John 1:7).

Fellowship always means sharing our lives with one another. We share our time, our joy, our suffering. We share our resources such as money, possessions, gifts and abilities with our brothers and sisters in faith. God's kingdom is real and must be expressed in a real way; that is to say in the flesh, in order to confess and honor the Christ who came in the flesh. If we cannot share our lives and our resources with our brothers and sisters, we will not put them at God's disposal, either.

> If anyone says, "I love God," yet hates his brother, he is a liar. For anyone who does not love his brother, whom he has seen, cannot love God, whom he has not seen.
>
> (1 John 4:20)

Let us not deceive ourselves: the genuineness of our love for Jesus is demonstrated primarily in our love for our brethren, and of course for other people as well. According to John's Gospel, this is the deepest concern of Jesus' heart,

> "If you obey my commands, you will remain in my love...My command is this: Love each other as I have loved you."
>
> (John 15:10, 12)

If we love Jesus, we will long to see His face. But until now He has apparently decided to reveal it primarily in the countenance of our brother. If we cannot see Jesus' face in the life of our brother, it will not become familiar to us. We can consider others better than ourselves only if we seek Jesus in the other, find Jesus' countenance in Him and honor Jesus in Him.

Day 89

DAILY CLEANSING

We must be cleansed daily from mistrust, bitterness, negative thoughts and words; plus the resultant accusations. Only then will our inner eyes grow in the ability to see Jesus' countenance in the lives of our brothers and our sisters. If we keep on forgiving and cleansing ourselves from all accusations toward each other, our relationships will not only allow Jesus' beauty and glory to shine out, but it will also protect us and become a bulwark which the enemy cannot so easily penetrate. Every accusation weakens us. It is an innate aspect of the devil's character, for he is "the accuser of our brethren" (Revelation 12:10 KJV). Accusations make us weak, ill and repulsive! But we are destined to bring God's thoughts and love to our brother, our sister and above all to our marriage partners. We are ordained to bring His love to our children and our parents.

As we know, love is not primarily a matter of the emotions. It is a decision to continue forgiving our neighbor daily for his offensive behavior toward us and toward God. "Your attitude should be the same as that of Christ Jesus" (Philippians 2:5). It may appear impossible to meet this challenge of Paul's: that of having the same attitude as Jesus, of whom it is written that "he loved his own to the end" (John 13:1, translated from the German Jerusalem Bible). In the face of the greatest need and darkness (the most momentous challenge of His life in the knowledge that His disciples would all leave and deny Him) He knelt down once again to wash their feet and gathered each one to His heart. He assured His disciples that His love for them would outlast everything. This attitude towards one another, says Paul, should also fill our hearts. How is this possible?

First, according to Romans 8:29, our calling as God's sons and daughters is to be transformed increasingly into the likeness of His beloved Son. God wants to knock at our neighbor's heart by opening a path to Him through our hearts. The cross was God's path through Jesus' heart, the route by which He came to bring men life and light. He wants to open a highway through our hearts, as well, in order to lead people to life and light.

Day 90

KNOW WHO WE ARE

We read in John 13:3ff. that Jesus humbled Himself before His disciples by washing their dirty and dusty feet. He was like a servant, knowing "that the Father had put all things under his power, and that he had come from God and was returning to God."

That is the secret! Jesus knew that He was the Son of God, amalgamating all dignity and majesty with all authority and honor. His identity and position were unambiguous. His calling to reveal the name of the Father was unequivocal. In this awareness of who He was, He could serve His disciples unconditionally, without expecting gratitude or any kind of authentication. He could give without having to receive. He could humble Himself and serve without losing His dignity because He was absolutely free from the need for reward and recognition. This kind of royal service sets men free. It cleanses, heals and transforms people into God's likeness. Such service is truly a royal discipline in God's kingdom.

A service which anticipates approval, appreciation and reward is degrading. It exposes the true motive of the servant and enslaves the one who is served because it binds him with demands and expectations. According to Romans 8:32, everything has been put in our hands, just as everything has been put in Jesus' hands:

He who did not spare his own Son, but gave him up for us all – how will he not also, along with him, graciously give us all things?

We have been given everything: dignity, an inheritance, our place in God's presence, honor and a calling. That is the prerequisite for growth in the same attitude as Jesus. For God has called us to be like Him in fidelity to our Father, in dedication to our brothers and sisters, in allegiance to our neighbors.

Day 91

ONE HEART AND ONE MIND

It is written of the first church, "All the believers were one in heart and mind...they shared everything they had" (Acts 4:32). This recalls Philippians 2:2, where Paul wrote to the church in Philippi, "make my joy complete by being like-minded, having the same love, being one in spirit and purpose."

Paul's profound concern, plus the description of the first church under the fresh work of the Holy Spirit, may appear somewhat utopian, if not other-worldly. We all know that where people live together, there is usually some form of a battle for existence in which each one attempts to promote himself, to meet his own needs and to ferret out confirmation. And yet Paul insists that those who belong to Jesus' family have absolutely no cause to oppose one another, to separate themselves out from one another or to live on their guard. On the contrary, we may and should care for one another. We should do everything possible on our part in order that others can experience kindness, care, counsel and admonition born of love and the fear of God.

Admonishing our brother does not mean drawing him to our convictions, our lifestyle or our culture. It entails pointing him to God's culture, to Jesus' lifestyle. That lifestyle is expressed in forgiveness, kindness, mercy, patience, truth and love. Admonishing does not mean judging, condemning, accusing or mistrusting. It means pointing to Jesus, without pressure, so that only Jesus' yoke will be laid on our neighbor. And "his yoke is easy."

Day 92

STREAMS OF LIVING WATER

It can be very challenging to dedicate ourselves completely to others so that they can taste God's love, for we disciples of Jesus are all in a process of inner restoration and we still need much inner healing. Jesus' likeness is often slow to take form in us. Therefore, when we set out to care for others we often come up against ingratitude, mistrust, disbelief, insincerity; even pride and arrogance. Then there is a great temptation to give up and turn away because we lose hope and faith for the other person. But the love to which we are called does not originate in the limits of our own human power. It is rooted in the unshakeable, strong and ultimately victorious love of a God who wants to access others through our hearts.

But this love can make a pathway only if our neighbor's reactions are unable to threaten or wound us. We develop sufficient stability only if we fill our heart daily with the awareness that Jesus not only knows us, but fully understands us. We read in Psalm 139:2, "you perceive my thoughts from afar." God knows our need for protection and security; He knows what we require for life. Our body, our soul and our spirit will lack nothing, because Jesus assures us in John 10:10 that He came to give us life to the full. A life-giving stream will flow from the heart of the one who is thus secure in God's love and care because he knows God's Word.

Just imagine if all of Jesus' disciples always encapsulated this attitude toward one another. Envisage streams of living water constantly flowing from all their hearts. What a fruitful garden the Church of God would be! The desert would bloom and God's glory and beauty would percolate everywhere.

Section 11

FORGIVENESS

"Forgive us our debts, as we have also forgiven our debtors."

(Matthew 6:12)

Day 93

ONLY HE WHO FORGIVES
WILL BE FORGIVEN

Do we realize what we are saying when we pray the Lord's Prayer? Are we really so bold as to ask God to forgive us as we have forgiven others? We have no choice. God Himself gave us this prayer and He makes it all even stronger in Matthew 6:15,

> "But if you do not forgive men their sins, your Father will not forgive your sins."

That hits home and raises the question why God is then so absolute, even so inflexible regarding forgiveness.

Forgiveness has to do with God's character, just as accusation and condemnation have to do with the devil's. In order to make it possible for a person to receive forgiveness, God let Himself be mocked. He "embraced" the total ugliness of the human heart – the vileness, the cowardice, the pride, the arrogance, the egoism, the apathy, the narrowness, hardness and self-righteousness. He struggled and suffered for men so that they could go out from the kingdom of evil, from accusation, condemnation and death and enter life, freedom and joy. He became the door. The end of death and the beginning of life, the end of despair and the beginning of hope, the end of hatred and the beginning of peace, the end of sorrow and the beginning of joy – this is forgiveness!

Forgiveness is the most precious gift we can receive or give. Receiving or giving forgiveness is like water in a dry and thirsty land. It is like a ray of sunshine on a gray, cold morning, like a piece of fresh bread after days of hunger. It is like a child's kiss before going to sleep, like the smile of a baby who stretches his arms out to us: pleasing, liberating and healing, bringing hope.

God's forgiveness is like a stream of water which makes the heart's desert blossom. But if this stream cannot flow forth it becomes a sewer which so stinks of self-righteousness and religious pride that our life becomes a stench of death. Receiving and giving forgiveness makes the heart wide and transforms bitter, hard and wounded hearts into soft, sympathetic, light and joyful hearts. Because our God is a God of life, peace, joy and hope, the hearts of all who call Him "Father" become a spring from which streams an aroma of life, flowing out to others and to the whole creation.

Day 94

FORGIVENESS LIBERATES US FOR LIFE

A person's ability to trust, to hope and to love is directly dependent on the measure of forgiveness he has received and granted to others. Forgiveness offers trust, hope and love. Jesus said, "But he who has been forgiven little loves little" (Luke 7:47). If we realize that it is difficult for us to accept ourselves and that we have little joy in our lives, it might be because we refuse to allow Jesus and our neighbor to forgive our failure and the ugliness of our hearts. And even if we know that Jesus forgives us, it might be that we refuse to forgive ourselves. If we do not accept the forgiveness which is offered for our sin, for our meanness, our maliciousness and cowardice, our egoism, our thoughtlessness, faithlessness and betrayal we will remain in a cold, dark prison. This prison will gradually suck all the life out of us and turn our heart into a stone.

Such a heart will not have a place at God's great end-time feast, for it will be a feast of joy, hope, trust, love and light.

Do we lack love for our neighbor? Is it difficult for us to offer him hope, trust and love? Is it difficult for us to keep on starting over with him because of his sin, weakness and failures? Then we must look at ourselves to see how ready we are to forgive. For the person who is willing to receive forgiveness, but not to give it, will end up like the evil servant whose million-dollar debt was cancelled but who had his debtor thrown into prison for a fifty-dollar debt (see Matthew 18:21-35).

We must acquit of all accusations those who wrong us and hurt us. We must keep on beginning anew with them, trusting them, reconciling ourselves with them without demanding our right to apology. Otherwise the forgiveness we have received will become a curse, as in the story of the evil servant. In the end he lost everything, even his life. God created for us access to life, freedom and joy through Jesus' blood. But He will have to cover His face in our presence, yes even turn from us, if we refuse others access to life, peace and freedom. No sin is too great for Jesus' blood to cleanse – unless we stubbornly refuse to accept or give forgiveness.

Day 95

WHAT FORGIVENESS IS
AND WHAT IT CAN DO

Before a close friend of mine became a Christian his life
was filled with drug dealing and with apathy and disrespect
toward others. This made him an unbearable person whose
icy heart was filled with arrogance. When he encountered
Jesus and was willing to admit his heart's ugliness and
guilt, God's forgiveness began transforming his heart into
a blooming garden with a stream of living water running
through it. He began loving people, nature and animals in a
new way.

One day a drug ring of which he had been a member
was broken. He was summoned to clarify his own
participation, and to be questioned as a witness. Jesus took
this opportunity to speak to him about his willingness to
admit his guilt, even before the law. For forgiveness can take
place only when a person steps totally into the truth, as we
read, "the truth will set you free" (John 8:32).

This friend realized he could no longer hide anything and
must admit the whole truth in order to live in full freedom.
He realized, furthermore, that this truth would bring him
several years in prison. But because he had tasted the power
of forgiveness he was willing to bear the consequences
of the truth. He sat alone with the examining judge, who

listened to his whole story for an hour. Then my friend was released with the comment, "You have fulfilled your duty and now have a clean conscience before the law. And now I will also do my duty." As the judge said this, he tore up the examination protocol! My friend went out a free man, feeling like a child at the beginning of the long summer vacation – no homework or duties, only time, water, sun and forest in front of him.

Day 96

A SECOND STORY ABOUT WHAT FORGIVENESS CAN BRING

Another good friend of mine worked for many years as a dedicated Christian in a group with other believers. Because God had given him many gifts and he brought more fruit than others, envy, ill-will and misunderstandings arose. In the end he was even slandered with insinuations until he left the group deeply wounded and disappointed, although he had contributed much.

After he had recovered, some time later, he put himself at God's disposal again and started a new ministry. But even there the same people persecuted him by spreading evil rumors in an attempt to hinder him in his new ministry. Bitterness and disappointment grew. He found so much opposition from his circle of former friends almost unbearable. Nevertheless, he continued building up his ministry – with some success, but also with a heavy heart. These un-reconciled relationships and the bitterness were like heavy stones he had to carry around the whole time.

As he spoke with God about this he kept insisting he was in the right. After all, he was the one who had been wounded and slandered. But God did not seem to be listening. One day the Lord spoke. "Look, it doesn't matter if you're in the right. If you want your ministry to have any meaning at all, then go and be reconciled with your brothers. Don't demand an apology and don't wait until they take the first step. But go, turn toward them again, offer your friendship, bless them, pray for them and help them wherever you can." With God's help my friend did just that. Although he was initially met with much mistrust and lack of understanding, the old friends came to realize that he was not accusing them. That made it possible for them to open their hearts. My friend told me that these friends now come to him when they need advice. Their mutual esteem is deeper than ever. This is what forgiveness can accomplish!

Section 12

KINGDOM LIFESTYLE

How good and pleasant it is
when brothers live together in unity!
It is like precious oil poured on the head,
running down on the beard,
running down on Aaron's beard,
down upon the collar of his robes.
It is as if the dew of Hermon were
falling on Mount Zion.
For there the Lord bestows his blessing,
even life for evermore.

(Psalm 133)

Day 97

OUR COMMISSION:
MAKING GOD'S KINGDOM VISIBLE

We are created in God's likeness and should mirror His character, His peace, His joy, His glory and beauty, His goodness and friendliness, His righteousness and faithfulness, so that His whole diversity will be visible in creation. Building God's kingdom in this world means making the reality of Jesus' rule visible and comprehensible through our lives. This is man's destiny and fulfillment.

When we sons and daughters of God are transformed into Jesus Christ's character, God's kingdom grows. At the same time, the kingdom of darkness is driven away. Psalm 133 promises life and blessing from the Lord where brothers – i.e. children of God – live in relationships that are pleasing to Him. As a fellowship of God's sons and daughters we are called to build His kingdom in us and through our mutual relationships. The revelation of God's reconciliation with man in Jesus should be visible in us. That is the goal and purpose of our lives.

Regarding God's kingdom, we keep returning to the same simple truths. If we had all abilities, all zeal, all discipline, all control, even if we had all human and spiritual authority, but had no love for God and our neighbor, our lives would be meaningless and empty in God's eyes (cf.

1 Corinthians 13:1-3). As endlessly diverse, creative and colorful as God's kingdom is, it is built on a very simple and unpretentious principle. This principle is so simple that Jesus said,

> "I praise you, Father, Lord of heaven and earth, because you have hidden these things from the wise and learned, and revealed them to little children."
>
> (Matthew 11:25)

God revealed it to the children, not to those who think highly of their own values and their own judgment regarding God and the world, those who ridicule God's Word and belittle it as utopian wishful thinking. What is absolutely essential to God is accessible not only to simple people, but to everyone who can bend down low enough. For His kingdom can develop only in a heart which is aware of its poverty and need and which confesses, "Lord, be merciful to me, a poor sinner!"

Day 98

CREATION'S GOAL

In order to gain a deep understanding of the basic ties between our personal relationship to God and our relationship to our neighbor – whom we are given so that by living with him our love for and relationship to God is made visible – it is important to study God's creation thoughts.

God created man to be a living reflection of His love, to be in His presence and to have fellowship with Him, for God is a God of relationships. Fellowship is thus neither an organization nor an institution, but an expression of living relationship. The goal of all creation was and is fellowship: fellowship of men with God, with each other and with all the rest of creation. God created man as a relational being, so only in a living relationship to his creator can he find his self-identity, his security, his peace and in fact everything which makes up his life. God created man in His image as a being who loves, for He wanted man to participate totally in His being. God's being is love. And love is revealed in relationships.

The Fall broke relationships on all levels. Man no longer oriented himself by God and His word. The consequence was that he conclusively lost every vital and life-preserving relationship: the relationship to God, to himself and to his neighbor. With that, he also lost his own identity and security. He forgot who he was, for a person with no relationships to others has no information about himself.

The world is still in this condition today and even we who are redeemed experience in our own lives the consequences of this great tragedy. Our relationships on all levels are more or less destroyed, unhealthy and un-clarified. We are driven by fear, egoism and obsession with self. Love for God is extinguished and the relationship to Him severed, making further fellowship impossible.

IN GOD'S LIGHT WE HAVE FELLOWSHIP

But God's goal is still fellowship. Therefore in Jesus He gave us an opportunity to find our way back to Him, the God of relationships, and to be born anew into this fellowship. Jesus said of Himself,

> "I am the light of the world. Whoever follows me will never walk in darkness, but will have the light of life."
>
> (John 8:12)

Whoever follows Jesus and is oriented toward Him will experience life and fellowship:

> if we walk in the light, as he is in the light, we have fellowship with one another, and the blood of Jesus, his Son, purifies us from every sin.
>
> (1 John 1:7)

Fellowship grows only to the extent that we live with each other and before each other in Jesus' light, i.e. the extent to which we become open toward each other with our whole being. Brotherly love (or fellowship) is possible only in the light. Love and light together protect us on the straight path to the Father.

Whoever loves his brother lives in the light, and there is nothing in him to make others stumble.

(1 John 2:10, translated from the German Luther Bibel, 1984)

If we are transparent and living in the light, genuine fellowship with every other person will be possible – no matter what his social status or cultural background.

The light reveals our own sinfulness, our guilt and our weakness. We can cope with this only if we let Jesus' blood cleanse us, if we receive forgiveness and if we forgive others. If we do not forgive our brother who has sinned against us – whether from ineptitude or misunderstandings – we are not building God's kingdom. Where we do not forgive or let go of our accusations against our brother, we unite ourselves with the accuser Satan. His being becomes visible in us. Yes, accusation attracts the enemy as manure attracts flies.

However, if forgiveness permeates our relationships, our Father and His kingdom will be seen in us. Therefore Jesus challenges us to pray,

"Forgive us our debts, as we also have forgiven our debtors."

(Matthew 6:12)

This is not simply a matter of reciprocal forgiveness. God wants His character to be visible in us – He who is merciful and compassionate and quick to forgive.

Day 100

RECONCILIATION MAKES
RELATIONSHIPS POSSIBLE

Jesus' most central concern was to lead us through His death back to before the Fall, back into a sound, perfect and total relationship to the Father. He reconciled us with the Father in order to make reconciliation with ourselves and with others possible. Reconciliation means turning toward one another, being aware of them again. Relationship and fellowship are fruits of reconciliation. We lose our fear and mistrust regarding others, making mutual openness possible. If we turn towards another, this also means accepting him as he is, with all his weaknesses. This makes possible deeply trusting relationships which are free of accusations and fear.

Destroyed relationships can be restored only when we are willing for the Holy Spirit to lead us into the truth – the truth about ourselves, about God and about our neighbor. "Search me, O God, and know my heart" (Psalm 139:23). God's Spirit must search us, lead us into the light and change us if we want to become ambassadors of reconciliation. Reconciliation is demanding and requires conscious living. We need God's Spirit to keep leading us into the truth about ourselves and to reveal where we are still ruled by accusations, bitterness and lack of reconciliation. Because we are still on the path to sanctification we must practice this reconciliation every day.

Shared lives and close relationships give each one of us opportunities to grow into reconciliation with ourselves, with our brothers, with our place and situation. With growing reconciliation, our accusations against God, our brother and ourselves will decrease in our lives and God's kingdom begins to grow in us.

Day 101

WHOEVER LOVES GOD,
LOVES HIS BROTHER AS WELL

Lasting community living is possible only if every participant cleanses his relationships daily and lives in truth and forgiveness. Whoever lives with others cannot long persist in lack of reconciliation without being discovered. Thus community living promotes God's kingdom in us. Jesus' character must become increasingly visible or we would not be able to stand each other. Therefore we work on ourselves and on our relationships. This is what makes spiritual counseling and biblical instruction so important. We do not seek to create a special spirituality, but to practice God's Word in our lives. This has a price and always begins with ourselves, like everything in God's kingdom. God has no employees who merely do their duty which they are paid for, but sons and daughters who testify to His nature and lordship through their very being in this world.

Through His sacrificial death Jesus led us to the place where we can practice the one commandment which is the fulfillment of the law and the prophets and all His plans. By restoring our relationship to God He makes us capable again of that for which we were created – love.

> "'Love the Lord your God with all your heart and with all your soul and with all your mind.' This is the first and greatest commandment. And the second is like it: 'Love your neighbor as yourself.'"
>
> (Matthew 22:37-39)

"The second is like it" means that love for our brother will always follow our love for God. The healthier our relationship to ourselves, the freer we are to approach our neighbor. John confirmed this,

> he has given us this command: Whoever loves God must also love his brother.
>
> (1 John 4:21)

Love is visible in the way we relate to our brother. In principle it is not possible to have a rich and vital relationship to God which is not expressed in our relationship to ourselves and to our brother.

Day 102

JESUS' LEGACY:
A NEW COMMANDMENT...

Community life is not a Christian extra for those who are especially called or gifted, but the very mark of Jesus' disciples. The legacy Jesus left us includes His words:

> "A new command I give you: Love one another. As I have loved you, so you must love one another. By this all men will know that you are my disciples, if you love one another."
>
> (John 13:34-35)

Others will not see that we are Jesus' disciples by our immaculate lives or by supernatural manifestations, but by the way we relate to one another. Our relationships will make God's kingdom visible and tangible. The goal of community life must always be to make Jesus known in this world so that people will talk about Him.

As soon as we decide to live in such relationships of light, whether in our family, our cell group or our work place we will be unavoidably confronted with the truth about ourselves and about each other. The narrow-mindedness, the lack of reliability, the egoism, the insistence on being right, the superficiality, yes, every area in which our brother needs healing will stare us in the face. (Of course, our brother will also experience this in his relationship to us!) But we will not really take on the burden of his life unless we are deeply concerned about him, i.e. if we no longer avoid him but care about him to the point where we make his life a part of our lives. Out of love for God and our brother we should become his "keeper" instead of turning away like Cain, saying, "Let everyone look after themselves!"

Paul knew the cost of brotherly love, of mutual relationships, very well. Therefore he said,

> Carry each other's burdens, and in this way you will fulfill the law of Christ.
>
> (Galatians 6:2)

The law of Christ is summarized in the double commandment of love (see Matthew 22:37-39). If we wish to fulfill it we will have to bear the burden of our brother. But here we are concerned not only with others' burdens: we must also let our own burden be carried; we must ask our brother to put up with us, without there being any distance between us or any masks. We cannot withdraw from him. In Jesus' light who we really are will also become visible to our brother, to the extent we allow this. Community life requires us to decide every day not to withdraw, not to hold back anything from our God or our brother. Then our lives will build and testify to God's kingdom.

Day 103

IN THIS WORLD, BUT NOT OF THIS WORLD

The world's motivation for fellowship is fundamentally different from the kingdom of God's. In the world fellowships are always created with a certain purpose in mind. People with common interests join together and profit from one another until their interests change and they part ways. Sympathy, gifts, knowledge, beauty or power play a major role. Relationships are chosen according to their usefulness. We need others in order to live.

Christian fellowship is, however, like a family into which we are born. We cannot choose our siblings. Fellowships created for a certain purpose can be dissolved at any time, but we cannot simply leave our families – as uncomfortable as this may sometimes be. Family relationships last in eternity.

What binds us as Jesus' disciples is that we belong to this family, regardless of any achievements. Gifts, interests and professional training are secondary. We do not meet together in order to receive life from one another, but to experience Jesus – who gives life – together.

Our motivation for relationships is not what the other person is like, but Jesus in Him. Because we receive our affirmation and our value from Jesus, others do not have to meet our needs. So we can set them free. God's kingdom becomes tangible when people bear one another out of love for Jesus, not out of mutual sympathy, and do not withdraw when weaknesses come to the fore.

In a fellowship oriented by Jesus' words, no one has to struggle for his place, his rights, his life or his value. On the contrary, we should submit to one another, meaning that we renounce every effort to promote our self-value; we concentrate on our brother. In community life we can practice looking away from ourselves daily. We can be thankful from our whole hearts for everything God put in our brother and developed in him. We learn from our brother without mentally calculating the areas in which we are superior. In this way we honor and respect Jesus in him, which does not mean we are blind to our brother's weaknesses or sins.

Day 104

RESPECTING AND
ADMONISHING OUR BROTHER

Community life stands and falls on the certainty that Jesus dwells in our midst and in the other's life. This creates a basic respect for our brothers and sisters, no matter what their background or abilities. We respect and love them for Jesus' sake. If we cannot respect our brother, we disdain Jesus as well. For in God's kingdom it is impossible to have a good relationship to Jesus and simultaneously disdain our brother. If we inwardly withdraw from our brother, Jesus will always be on his side. Our behavior toward our brother reflects our true attitude toward our Lord. In shared living, this is more visible than anywhere else.

We often think the other person is too one-sided, too uninteresting, too haughty, too immature and much more. We lose sight of Jesus in him. God must point out the veracity of our relationships because we fallen persons have lost all sense of reality in ourselves and in our neighbor. God wants us to respect one another, whether the other is a leader or a newcomer. The decisive thing is that Jesus lives in him. Not one of us is worthy of love because of our own selves. What is worthy of love in us is always Jesus.

In Galatians 6:1 we read, "Brothers, if someone is caught in a sin, you who are spiritual should restore him gently."

This means that we should uncover sin in our relationships and should not shy away from calling it by name – but always with respect, without exposing the other person. We have no right to reject him for this. When we admonish, our brother should experience our unconditional love for him. We must differentiate between the sin and the sinner. Every one of us must realize that we ourselves are also capable of every sin which others have committed. This awareness will help us remain merciful.

Only from a reconciled, healthy relationship to God will it be possible to seek our brother for his own sake – without secretly thinking we can use him for something.

Day 105

COMMUNITY LIFE CREATES LIVING SPACE

Psalm 133 makes clear that God is pleased when His children care for one another and share their lives in unity. Then He sends blessing, life of everlasting quality. Is this not what we really desire and attempt to somehow attain with all the powers of our imaginations?! "Live together," as it says in verse 1, does not necessarily mean that we live in the same house or the same town. This is much more a matter of the quality and depth of our relationships. People living in the way God is talking about are very familiar with each other; they come and go in each other's lives and homes. One person's life really affects the other's; no one can be apathetic. Our brother's well-being, his relationship to God, his daily life, his paths concern us. They lead us to thoughtful care, to prayer, to bearing the other's burden and to action. God will respond with His pleasure and His blessing to all this sharing and mutual concern. He Himself will create life and living space for all concerned.

This living space grows, for example, when we experience our brother's care and love. Seeing that others stand by us, seek us and accept us creates security. God's love becomes very tangible through our brother; trust grows in God and in our brothers and sisters. This relaxes and liberates us so that we can let go of the obstinate battles for our own lives, for recognition, for confirmation; we can give up our fear of coming up short. We will have the same experience as the psalmist who wrote,

> In my anguish I cried to the Lord,
> and he answered by setting me free.
>
> (Psalm 118:5)

Our horizons will be broadened when our brother demonstrates to us the extent to which God accepts, loves, esteems and knows us. Of course God can also reveal this directly to our hearts. But He wants His love to become flesh through us for our brother, and for us through our brother.

Day 106

COVERING THE OTHER'S NAKEDNESS

Living space is also created when we fully open ourselves to our brother, confident that he will continue to love us even when he discovers our sin, mistakes and weaknesses. In order to make such openness possible we need a clear framework of commitment to others. We must formulate agreements such as discretion and a determination to keep making new starts with each other and to live before each other in truth and openness. Only in a house whose windows and doors are well insulated can warmth be developed. Even then we need courage and resolve to allow others to see behind the very private curtains of our everyday lives, i.e. to live in this light of which 1 John 1:7 speaks.

By nature we are too cowardly to really admit what is inside us, for fear of rejection. So we try to hide or draw attention away from us. But within a defined group of brothers and sisters our lives will become public to a certain degree if we have decided to share them. In the framework of this binding common life, our insecurities, fears and weaknesses can come to the light because our brother demonstrates Jesus' unconditional love, which will not withdraw from us even then. Nakedness can be revealed without humiliation or withdrawal because it will be covered by our brothers. Thus our dignity will be preserved.

Day 107

WHOEVER LOSES HIS
LIFE WILL FIND IT...

When we decide to commit ourselves to one another we must at the same time renounce the right to our own private sphere and to individualism, which serve the illusion that we ourselves are able to create our own living space. This has its price for all of us because there are no born "fellowship types." We are all born individualists, whatever the reasons. On the natural level, every person attempts to create his own living space according to his opportunities and personal ideals. These include material goods, free time, education, knowledge, Christian activities, hobbies, a special service or relationships. But all these things we can possess on earth we will one day have to leave behind. They are not part of the eternal life spoken of in Psalm 133. Life in eternity has nothing to do with possessions, but with the experience of God's care through our brother. This care changes our hearts and makes us confident that God is for us. Even when the brother is no longer present we can stand on the foundation of this experience, reconciled with life.

The goal of community life and of brotherly love in action is always to reveal Jesus and to make God the sole source of our lives. Committed fellowship will lead the individual to an ever-deeper relationship with God, not to dependence on men, as some object. For in the long run, community living increasingly reveals the brother's inadequacy as well as our own weaknesses. Then we need God's grace all the more so that we can accept the other in spite of his "incorrigible" weaknesses.

The genuineness of every Christian fellowship is revealed in the extent to which its members grow into a mature, independent and deep relationship to God, the Father; the extent to which this relationship nourishes their lives so they can testify to Jesus in this world.

Day 108

COMMUNITY LIFE SETS
US FREE TO SERVE

The Holy Spirit creates the experience of reconciliation with God, with ourselves and with our neighbor; He heals our relationships and gives us inner living space. Even when we experience all of this in our relationships to our brothers and sisters, when we encounter God's love in them, it is still the Holy Spirit Himself who creates this reconciliation and breadth.

The Holy Spirit's goal is always to build and spread God's kingdom. By beginning with our own hearts He prepares us for service. Community life itself is not the goal, nor does it consist solely of personal healing. Just as we are called to mutual love, so we are also called to seek and save the lost. The world should see Jesus in us.

When the question of our own value is clarified, we will be increasingly capable of every type of service. In trusting, committed fellowship our hearts will one day grasp that our value is based solely on God's love for us. It is not what we have amassed, neither riches nor gifts nor whatever others think or say of us. God the Father is the only one who has the right to grant us our identity.

Life in the light has taught us to move in freedom and without fear. If we have revealed ourselves to our brothers and sisters, we have nothing more to lose. Then the path is free for relationships and friendship with all sorts of persons, no matter what our own experiences or personal sympathies.

Day 109

POWERFUL TESTIMONY

By sharing our lives with one another we will learn to know God better and better and will be led closer to His heart. At His heart we will not only experience security for our own lives, but He will also give us a vision for others who, although strangers to us, are close to God. Being close to the Father's heart is the only thing which can create in us the desire to go and tell those who are lost, lonely, cold and in prison the good news that God loves them. We will be motivated by God's love for them. We will not have to be full-time servants, such as missionaries or pastors. In every firm, in every office, on every construction site, in every shop and every neighborhood are countless people living in darkness, loneliness and fear of death. Every day can be an occasion to share this good news with them.

It is not primarily our theological knowledge which makes us capable of sharing Jesus with others: it is our heart relationship to the Father and the experience that in Jesus He has given us everything.

If we encounter God's enemy he will not ask how fluent or bold we are. He will first put his finger on our own lives and rightly ask, "What about your relationship to your God, to yourself and to your brothers and sisters?" If he finds accusations, hopelessness and lack of reconciliation in our lives, he will easily be able to pressure us and lay his hand

– with its paralyzing and binding reality – on our lives. He will not take us seriously.

The devil fears people who live in forgiveness because he cannot draw them into mistrust, bitterness or hatred. Those who are willing to forgive spread a stench of death for the devil. The way we treat others will show him whose children we are and in whose name we act. This name alone gives us protection and authority to move in the kingdom of darkness.

Section 13

LIGHT IN THE DARKNESS

"Arise, shine, for your light has come,
and the glory of the Lord rises upon you.
See, darkness covers the earth
and thick darkness is over the peoples..."

(Isaiah 60:1-2)

Day 110

WHAT IS DARKNESS?

Most Christians are very familiar with the subject of light. Most of us have already heard numerous sermons on this central theme of the gospel. If we wish to think about light in the darkness we must first clarify the concepts and emotions we associate with these two terms.

In our family we celebrate the beginning of the Sabbath, Erev Sabbath, every week. In this important family ceremony, we close the week together and bless each other by expressing God's thoughts over one another. The mother is especially honored for her often hidden dedication to all of us; we read Proverbs 31:10-31 to her. After she has lit the candles and said the blessing – thanking God that He has called us through salvation in Christ to be a light in the world – it is our custom for each person at the table to recite a Bible verse about light. This reminds us of what it means that we are called to be light, as the Lord said in Isaiah 42:6, "I will...make you...a light for the Gentiles."

In the parable of the wedding banquet (Matthew 22:1-14) Jesus speaks about darkness. The guests who were invited didn't come, so the king sent his servants out onto the streets to invite people. But evidently one of them wasn't wearing the prescribed wedding clothes. This made the king so angry that he commanded, "throw him outside, into the darkness, where there will be weeping and gnashing of teeth" (v. 13b). Jesus sometimes used this expression to describe the place assigned to those whose attitude blocked access to the table of Abraham, Isaac and Jacob, i.e. fellowship with God and with those who belong to Him.

> "[M]any will come from the east and the west, and will take their places at the feast with Abraham, Isaac and Jacob in the kingdom of heaven. But the subjects of the kingdom will be thrown outside, into the darkness, where there will be weeping and gnashing of teeth."
>
> (Matthew 8:11-12)

The darkness is obviously a condition in which men are absolutely incapable of perceiving God's presence. But whoever is cut off from God is cut off from life, from peace, from joy, from light, from fellowship – in short from everything it means to be a human being.

Day 111

JESUS, THE LIGHT OF THE WORLD

Darkness is the condition of man without God; and whoever is without God is ultimately without his fellow men as well. Whoever cannot perceive God will also be estranged from man, who is made in God's image. He will neither know nor understand him, leading to absolute isolation. Darkness is isolation. Therefore it cannot surprise us that the world, which is covered in darkness, suffers increasingly from isolation. This disease manifests itself as depression, addictions, inability to relate to others, or loud violence and rebellion against everything and everyone – all to avoid being alone with oneself in the darkness.

Whoever knows God is never isolated because God surrounds him (see Psalm 139:5). Whoever doesn't live in God's presence doesn't live in the light, and whoever doesn't live in the light lives in darkness and isolation. For it is written,

> If we walk in the light, as he is in the light, we have fellowship with one another, and the blood of Jesus, his Son, purifies us from all sin.
>
> (1 John 1:7)

Jesus is the light of the world and God's presence in the world. Without the light of God's presence, a man cannot really find his fellow human beings. He cannot build up and motivate others. In order to promote things which make our neighbor's life worth living – peace, joy, security, healthy self-value, an identity rooted in God – we need qualities which Ephesians 5:9 names "the fruit of light." The first of these is goodness, meaning warmth of the heart, then mercy, patience, friendliness, generosity. Without light, the opposite of goodness reigns: mistrust, envy, bitterness, narrow-heartedness, coldness, judging and condemning. Truth is also a fruit of the light. Without light, slander, distortion of facts and half-truths reign. Where there is no light, forgiveness is neither given nor received.

An additional fruit of light is justice. In the world – and, unfortunately, often among us Christians as well – justice is defined according to achievements, abilities, wealth and inherited privileges. Of course we know that we're all equal before the law. But even when equal justice is given to all, its egalitarianism often violates the individual's circumstances. God's righteousness, on the other hand, judges and directs us. It sets us in the right relationship to God, to ourselves and to our neighbor. Because God knows our soul to its depths (Psalm 139:13), only His justice can give us the care and position suited to our being and our reality.

Day 112

I AM A LIGHT!?

What does light have to do with those of us who consider ourselves Jesus' disciples? It is important to be clear about the foundation on which we stand, for Lucifer, the demon of darkness, also wants to be seen as an angel of light and he is very successful at it. Billions of people follow this pseudo-light. They get lost under the rule of darkness and destruction and perish there. From the Dalai Lama to Mohammed, from Javier Solana to Kofi Annan – all want to be seen as light-bearers, as signposts to true humanness. The world is full of false lights which lead to the abyss.

But Jesus says, "I am the light of the world" (John 8:12). We believe that Jesus, and Jesus alone, is the absolute revelation of God. Jesus is the visible God who became flesh. Nowhere else can we know or see who God really is and what He is really like, as written in John's Gospel,

> "No one has seen God at any time. The only begotten Son, who is in the bosom of the Father, He has declared Him."
> (John 1:18 NKJV)

When Jesus calls Himself "the light of life," He means the light which makes God's life-creating presence visible. Israel's calling must also be understood in this sense. Israel is to be a light for the nations, i.e. it is called to be a place where God reveals Himself to the peoples. It is easy for us to believe that Jesus is the light of the world. But what about Jesus' claim on His disciples' lives, as we read in Matthew 5:14, "You are the light of the world. A city on a hill cannot be hidden"?

Who of us could say unequivocally, "I follow Jesus and am therefore a light in this world; like Jesus, I make God's forgiving, life-creating and restoring presence visible to my neighbor. Whoever follows my example will come out of the darkness and find the living God and life"!? We usually relativize this, modestly pointing out our weaknesses, problems and inadequacies, so that we won't seem arrogant. Of course there are arrogant people who make themselves the standard, who take what they don't deserve, who lift themselves above things they don't understand, who judge and condemn what they don't know. But we cannot simply take it upon ourselves to be light. Either we are light or we are not. We become light by being ignited with fire.

Day 113

FALSE MODESTY

This is also the problem with our so-called modesty as Jesus' disciples. Such modesty is often nothing but spiritual evasion. We try our best to avoid light's claim on our lives because we shy away from the healing but painful process of being ignited and penetrated with fire. If we confess that Jesus is our Lord, we are children of God and thus light of the world. And Jesus says, "One doesn't light a lamp and put it under a bowl, but one puts it where everyone can see it" (cf. Matthew 5:15).

The calling to be light is an unpleasant and challenging demand on the darkness in our own lives. If we actually claim to be light in this world, the game of hide-and-seek is at an end. We can no longer withdraw to our own homes and think no one has a right to see into our lives. We can no longer say that our lives – our goals, our relationships, what we do with our money – concern no one else. Light makes things transparent. If we want to make God's heart visible for others, our own hearts must also be visible and tangible for them. Being light has grave consequences.

Our lives suddenly concern the world and this world even has a right to look into them! A city on a hill cannot be hidden. Our problem as Jesus' disciples is that of course we would love to be on the road with Him, but preferably just the two of us. We'd like to be in a secret place where no one finds out who we are or what we're doing. Otherwise we could be held accountable for our conduct! But that is exactly what Jesus means when He says, "You are the light of the world." We are the ones sent into the darkness so that God's kingdom can take hold in this world through us, driving away the darkness.

Day 114

UPSETTING THE DARKNESS

It is no small thing to enter the darkness. The darkness hates and opposes the light with all its means. All the pride, arrogance, greed, impurity, self-complacency, cowardice, untruthfulness and other negative characteristics which the darkness has developed in our lives and in the world do not want to be revealed! Whenever we refuse to submit to the saving judgment of God's Son, we will resist the light with all our strength.

But God wants us to be so penetrated by His truth and with the testimony of His Son, the crucified and risen overcomer of darkness, that we can influence this world which doesn't know Him. We should not only challenge the darkness, but dispel it and overturn it, because the darkness must yield! In order for this to happen, the light must have power. Power comes through the Holy Spirit's presence in our lives. He creates the fruits of light – kindness, justice, truth, forgiveness, love, as we read in the letters to the Ephesians and to the Galatians. Then people around us will see God's character.

Kindness means viewing others favorably, accepting their shortcomings instead of judging them – knowing that God is greater than their problems and that He has a path for them, too. A kind person doesn't give up on anyone because it is God's kindness that leads you toward repentance

(Romans 2:4). God's kindness never tires of inviting us to forgiveness and to life. It keeps on saying, "There is hope for you, there is a path, there is help. You aren't a hopeless case, no matter how overwhelmed and devastated you may be." This is a fruit of the light in the hopelessness of darkness!

Truth is another fruit of the light. But truth has a very unpleasant side. It distinguishes between light and darkness, between right and wrong, between the will of God and the will of man. It sets clear boundaries and creates barriers when necessary. We all too quickly relativize the truth of God's Word, according to the spirit of the times and the contemporary societal norms, because we fear the attacks which a clear profile would provoke. But if we don't orient ourselves by God's Word regarding sex, money, responsibility, power and influence, we will have nothing with which to oppose the darkness because we are part of it.

But if, out of love for the Jewish and the Arab peoples, as well as for our own nation, we confess, "The truth is not a thing but a person, namely Jesus the Messiah; no one can come to the heavenly Father except through Him," we will experience not only opposition and mockery but also resistance, exclusion and myriad forms of persecution. For darkness always reacts to light. We testify to others not out of arrogance or because we think we know everything better. We do it from obedience to God's Word, from the love and mercy we ourselves have experienced. We declare that there is something which cannot be discussed or compromised, namely that Jesus alone is the truth.

Day 115

CONFESSING JESUS TO THE JEWISH PEOPLE

Jesus is the truth which took on flesh and He is the only hope for the world. We are light in the darkness if we confess this with our whole lives, holding nothing back. For those of us who live as a community among the Jewish people – sharing our lives with them and bringing them daily to God's throne because we believe in God's faithfulness to them – it is always painful to meet Christians who conceal from them that Jesus is the only truth, sometimes even renouncing Him. They want to protect themselves from conflict with Jewish people. But withholding Jesus from the Jewish people is the greatest disservice we can do to them! For the good news of the incarnated grace and truth belongs to this people before any others. In Romans 1:16 God's Word says,

> I am not ashamed of the gospel, because it is the power of God for the salvation of everyone who believes: first for the Jew, then for the Gentile.

The gospel belongs first to the Jews so that they can know that the God of Israel revealed Himself and His name in Jesus Christ.

"I have made you known to them, and I will continue to make you known in order that the love you have for me may be in them and that I myself may be in them."

(John 17:26)

Therefore Jesus also says,

"I am the way and the truth and the life. No-one comes to the Father except through me."

(John 14:6)

It is exactly this message which is first for the Jews and then for all other peoples as well.

So if we want to be light in the darkness, in a place which doesn't know God, our whole lives must testify that we have no other answer; we have nothing to offer except the gospel, namely Jesus. It may sound easy to say that Jesus died for our sake, in order to save us from death and darkness; Jesus is risen and sits at God's right hand; He will return to take us to Himself and to judge the living and the dead; He is the answer to all questions, the hope in every situation. But let us begin testifying to Jesus as clearly as this, even in our immediate surroundings, and we will find out what it means to be a light.

Day 116

THE WORLD HUNGERS FOR LIGHT

How this world hungers for light! I am deeply grateful to God for my co-workers who keep on setting out. I cannot say that they never get tired, for they do. But we set out anyway in order to be light in the darkness. We go to men and women, to many children and youth – in the Islamic ghettos of Marseille and in Jerusalem, especially in the old city. How many children are growing up there in deepest darkness, in a godlessness filled with hatred and violence! In this darkness we are a light to them by testifying not only with words, but also through our relationships. We let them feel that God loves them, that they have a Father, that Jesus came to take them out of their life-destroying environment.

There aren't many whose lights shine into this darkness. That is why darkness is increasing. Enmity between the Jewish and the Arab peoples is spreading. But also in Switzerland, in Europe and in the whole world, lawlessness, egoism, apathy and godlessness are growing. They are devouring the souls of those for whom God's Son gave His life! Will we take up the challenge of our calling to be light in the world in Jesus' name? Or will we one day have to hear God's reproach and be ashamed that we let Him down, as the prophet Isaiah saw, "I looked, but there was no-one to help, I was appalled that no-one gave support" (Isaiah 63:5).

There is a price for being light in the darkness. Light always illumines us first. We must be examined because God wants our own lives to express light. Everyone who begins to say, "I want to be a light" will experience that God goes through his own life first, illuminating his relationships. We can fool each other about many things, but we can't fool God about anything. Nor can we fool the darkness. If we are not light in deed and in truth – because, for example, our relationships are not genuine and there is still bitterness in our own lives – the light will have to penetrate our own darkness. The darkness cannot be driven out by a vague piety.

God will arrange our priorities so that we can be light. What are our priorities? What are our life goals? And how are they different from the goals of people who don't know God? Is God's kingdom visible in our goals? It is important to ask ourselves these questions so that our lives will really push back the darkness and draw men into God's kingdom.

Day 117

THE COST OF LIVING IN THE LIGHT

We have an incredible message! Jesus, God's Son, came to seek what was lost, to save what would perish, to bring home what was led astray. It is a message worth giving our lives for because it is the only thing which can save the world! It is very important to God that His people Israel and all the peoples of the world hear and understand the gospel. The parable of the tenants in Matthew 21:33-39 makes clear what it cost Him: He not only turned His own Son over to darkness and death in order to destroy the works of the darkness, He also keeps on sending His servants, even though many of them are still being beaten, mistreated, or even killed. Up to the present day Jesus' disciples risk not only their comfort, their career, their personal desires and goals, their security and safety – but their lives as well. Because others have done exactly that before us, we can now know the good news.

What do we ourselves do, what do our friends, parents and congregations do, when God calls us to be a light in the darkness – perhaps even in dangerous and costly (including the financial cost) places?! Isn't such a calling often frustrated when we begin considering the security and cost? Who is willing to take the responsibility when those who were sent are beaten, mistreated and possibly killed? Who wants to invest in an undertaking which ends in failure and without visible results, like the servants in our parable? God does! We, on the other hand, are all too often led by our intellect and our desire for security. But God is led by His passion to save whatever can be saved.

Being light in the darkness has its price at all times and in every place. It isn't any easier in Switzerland than in Israel or in Afghanistan. And if the cost isn't as high in Switzerland, we must ask ourselves to what extent the light truly shines in the darkness. For we all surely agree that darkness exists in Switzerland and in the formerly Christian Occident.

Do we want to be light? Are we willing to fulfill this commission of Jesus? His commission is not only found in Matthew 28:19, "Go and make disciples of all nations," but even before that in His words in Matthew 5:14,

> "You are the light of the world. A city on a hill cannot be hidden."

We are light, we must therefore become visible!

This is what motivates our community. We want the Jewish people to see in our lives that the God of Israel is a living God and that in Jesus He came to His people and into this world. Of course we aren't accepted everywhere with open arms. Our community has experienced many situations in which we felt tempted to give it all up. But God reminded us that there is no fruit in eternity without the possibility that it may cost us our lives.

> "[U]nless a grain of wheat falls to the ground and dies, it remains only a single seed. But if it dies, it produces many seeds."
>
> (John 12:24)

Day 118

LORD, WHAT DO YOU WANT ME TO DO?

We all often ask, "Lord, what do You want from me?" We ask what our calling is and what God may want from us. May God illumine our lives? May He re-arrange our priorities? May He call us to a lifestyle which really upsets the darkness? May He call us out of our hiding place and make us public so that people can see Jesus in us? May He take us out of our routine? May He lead us out of our fears and shine His light into the areas where we don't yet know Him?

The world, especially the Islamic world, is waiting for the sons and daughters of God to become visible! Children, women, men who are longing for God but do not know Him are waiting for people to come and testify with their lives to His kindness, truth and mercy – to make God visible in a way which satiates the hungry.

I want to strongly admonish all of us: if you hear His voice in any area today, do not postpone your answer! Remember Hebrews 3:15, "Today, if you hear his voice, do not harden your hearts." This is often the seat of our problem. We ask God over and over again about His will and His path for our lives. But when He speaks to us, we begin to question His words. We can do this, to be sure. God does not force anything on us. But then we might continue asking for the rest of our lives what God wants from us.

God is waiting for us to answer, "Yes, Lord, I heard, I understood, I will obey. I'll take this seriously, even if it's costly, even if I'm not always understood and suddenly become an outsider." What does God desire more than for us to finally become outsiders and if necessary become fools for Jesus' sake! God is waiting for us to answer Him. Then He will show us what it means to be a light in the darkness. Moreover, God will share His joy with us when people suddenly recognize Him. It's worth investing everything for the sake of God's joy when Jesus' light shines in people's hearts!

The message we bring is not our own message. It is the message of the God of Israel who has called us to share the inheritance of believing Israel: to be a light in the world. We are all called to be this light in the darkness. It is not a question of talent, position or profession. Jesus called ordinary people to be light, not the specialists. It means that all of us are the light of the world, God's light in the darkness.

Section 14

YOU ARE MY WITNESSES

"[Y]ou will receive power when the Holy Spirit comes on you; and you will be my witnesses…"

(Acts 1:8)

Day 119

EVERYONE NEEDS JESUS

God is looking for witnesses, people who themselves have experienced His healing, liberating, peace-making and saving work; people who have heard, seen and felt the good news. Because God loves this world He let His Son Jesus descend into the darkness to create a path to life, freedom and peace. God is looking for people who proclaim that He, the creator of the universe, handed over His own heart to the world in His Son. Now we who follow our own ways and are lost in fear, darkness and death can find the way back home, as written in Isaiah 53:6,

> "We all, like sheep, have gone astray,
> each of us has turned to his own way;
> and the Lord has laid on him the iniquity of us all."

Going our own way means we revolve only around ourselves, around our own needs, rights, desires and problems. As we know, egoism turns every life into a prison of loneliness, despair and emptiness. Egoism makes us guilty toward ourselves, toward others and toward God. This is true not only of those who have not yet entered God's kingdom, but often of those who consider themselves Jesus' disciples as well. We, too, can go astray on our own egotistical paths;

then we need the love and care of brothers and sisters who help us find our way back to the Father's house.

But not everyone – not even every believer – who is following his own path realizes that he is lost and wandering. Many don't want to hear that without God's mercy man is lost and heading for destruction.

> "There is a way that seems right to a man,
> but in the end it leads to death."
>
> (Proverbs 16:25)

We wander through life's darkness on our self-chosen path which ultimately leads to death. Whoever has been touched by the gospel and thus found his way home will set out to seek the lost and to proclaim God's message of salvation. But he will encounter the tragedy that our proud, independent and wayward hearts often bluntly reject God's kindness, ignore it or mock it.

At these times it is often tempting to withdraw and leave people to their own fate and desires. It is one thing to bring the message to people who want to hear it. But Jesus died on the cross even for those who rejected, hated and opposed Him. He died for His enemies.

> "I offered my back to those who beat me,
> my cheeks to those who pulled out my beard;
> I did not hide my face from mocking and spitting."
>
> (Isaiah 50:6)

Day 120

YOU ARE THE LIGHT OF THE WORLD

Those of us who wish to bear witness to His message must constantly keep in mind that the witnesses to God's seeking love always had the same experiences. They were discouraged and tempted to give up or retreat in the face of rejection, exclusion, beatings or even murder. Jesus warned His disciples, "you will be hated by all nations because of me" (Matthew 24:9). But they also received God's help. And those who remain resolutely faithful to their commission to witness will be rewarded with the experience that God attains His goal. The lost will be found and the homeless will find their way back home.

Many have the impression that being a witness requires specific talents or education and therefore does not necessarily pertain to every disciple of Jesus. Of course education is helpful; it is also true that not every person is gifted and called to be an evangelist. But every person who says that Jesus, the light of the world, lives in his heart is a witness.

Everyone with the light of the world living in his heart becomes a light-bearer. Jesus said to all His disciples, "You are the light of the world" (Matthew 5:14). You and I – disciples of Jesus – are the light of the world. What a statement! Let's be honest. Most decent people are upset by this. Our healthy sense of humility demands that we relativize it if we don't wish to be considered arrogant. We disciples are the light of the world?

We don't need much knowledge of history to ask if it wasn't just this self-understanding amongst Christians which brought so much distress and misery on the world. We disciples of Jesus are an elite troop of good people? That would be a tragic misunderstanding. To whom was it said, "You are the light of the world"? To those who stood under Jesus' cross and accepted the verdict that there is no one righteous, not even one; no one who does good, no one who seeks God (see Romans 3:10-11). God chose the lowly, those with nothing to show, those who came up short, the unimportant, the weak in body, soul and spirit (see 1 Corinthians 1:27-28). Whoever considers himself one of these and comes to the cross daily will be brought into the light by Him who said, "I am the light of the world."

Only under the cross can Jesus fill our inner loneliness, restlessness and fears with His security, warmth, hope and peace. Whoever constantly makes room in his heart for this light will find that not only is his own heart satiated, but a stream of living water will flow out of him, dispensing warmth and hope to others.

Day 121

DO WE TESTIFY TO HOPE?

"You are My witnesses," says Jesus. We witness that the Son of God came to seek the lost and bring them home; that He came to lead us out of darkness and death; that there is a living hope and therefore all suffering, all misery, fear and violence will come to an end.

> "Now the dwelling of God is with men...There will be no more death or mourning or crying or pain, for the old order of things has passed away." He who was seated on the throne said, "I am making everything new!" Then he said, "Write this down, for these words are trustworthy and true."
>
> (Revelation 21:3-5)

This is the quintessence of our hope!

The world – and often we ourselves – connects the term "hope" with wishful thinking, in the way that the German proverb cited earlier does: "Hoping and persevering makes one a fool." But God's Word says the exact opposite: "hope does not disappoint us" (Romans 5:5) and "he who stands firm to the end will be saved" (Matthew 10:22). The proverb and the Bible testify to truths which are diametrically opposed to each other. Whichever one we believe reveals what kind of ground our lives are anchored into – for the Bible speaks of hope as an anchor for the soul (Hebrews

6:19).What is our testimony concerning the anchor of our souls? As Jesus' disciples, do we testify to this hope in the midst of our lives' storms – in the midst of illness, unemployment, relational conflicts, financial problems, even war and crime? Do we testify of hope to our congregations when they are shaken by events, when spiritual stagnation causes a crisis of faith? Do we testify of hope to unbelieving colleagues, friends and relatives who are in obvious trouble but not seeking help from the living God and His Messiah? Do we testify of hope for our country, our people?

What is the basis of our hope when we ourselves are wandering in a desert, when we are disappointed by other believers or rejected and misunderstood by the world? If our hope is based on faith in the goodness of man, or in other believers' friendship and integrity, we will eventually be disappointed. In the heart of man – even a believing man – there is nothing which gives reason for hope. For it is written, "Every inclination of his [man's] heart is evil from childhood" (Genesis 8:21).

Day 122

THERE IS HOPE ONLY IN JESUS

In Hebrews 6:18-19 we read,

> We who have fled to take hold of the hope offered to us may be greatly encouraged. We have this hope as an anchor for the soul, firm and secure.

The anchor of hope for our soul, the hope which can resist all the adversities of life, is Jesus alone. He is hope in person. He will renew everything. As He says of Himself,

> He has sent me to bind up the broken-hearted,
> to proclaim freedom for the captives
> and release from darkness for the prisoners,
> to proclaim the year of the Lord's favor
> and the day of vengeance of our God,
> to comfort all who mourn....
>
> (Isaiah 61:1-2)

What a message for our day! We needn't be prophets to see that our time is characterized by a great decay of biblical values and by the increase of violence, crime, apathy, egoism and lack of relationships. Economic and existential fears are like paralyzing vapors permeating our lives. As witnesses to the God of the Bible we can counter this perspective with the message that God creates a new beginning. He transforms fear into confidence, resignation into hope, war into peace, guilt and bitterness into forgiveness and salvation, mourning into joy, death into life.

Isaiah 61 clearly expresses the message of the year of the Lord's favor. Through His Messiah Jesus, God turns toward His people Israel and toward all of creation. He offers us a new beginning. Guilt is cancelled, prisoners of every kind released, relationships set in order; mercy is granted instead of justice, and grace instead of judgment.

God wants to send us to witness and to be a light; to make visible, audible and tangible the message that the biblical God is a God of grace, a God whose whole being is merciful. Those who are inwardly and outwardly imprisoned long for liberation; the broken-hearted and enslaved long for healing and restoration; the disappointed, resigned and hopeless for comfort, encouragement and reorientation.

The inwardly and outwardly poor are waiting to hear that God loves them and has called them to a life of peace and joy. God wants to halt the need, fear and darkness in everyone's life; He wants to create something new. The message of the year of favor is all-encompassing. It is the only answer to all the cries for salvation from pain and suffering. It is the only message which does not make fools of the hopeless.

"Whom shall I send?" God asks in Isaiah 6:8. Which of us who have experienced this message in our own lives will go for Him? How many will answer like the prophet Isaiah, "Here I am, send me!" (Isaiah 6:8). God is waiting for His joyous message to be brought to billions of people. How many of us disciples of Jesus – congregation members, congregation leaders, youth leaders, young, old – will respond to God's call and let ourselves be sent or support others who are sent out with this message? Or are we so far from God's mercy that we are no longer touched when people for whom Jesus gave His life continue getting lost on their own path and perishing in darkness?

Day 123

THE KERNEL OF WHEAT MUST DIE

Every year impressive and expensive conferences are held which encourage the participants to make genuine and decisive commitments to Jesus and to God's kingdom. They attempt to mediate understanding for the good news of God's reconciliation with man; understanding that this message of grace and a new beginning must be carried out to a world which is hurtling toward its own destruction.

But what are the fruits of these efforts? How many hearts are opened to God's call and answer, "Here I am, send me!"? How many men, women and youths decide to renounce their professional careers, the founding of a secure home, or even a Christian career in their home country? How many will fall into a field somewhere as a kernel of wheat; a kernel which must be broken apart so that those living in darkness can have the fruit of mercy, grace and light?

After these conferences won't the huge pile of kernels be returned to their secure, warm homes, where they will be stored and saved? At the same time the field outside is increasingly desolated and overgrown with weeds; the desert of godlessness covers and suffocates the last bit of receptive earth!

But God speaks not only to conference participants. How often during the course of our lives has He asked, "Will you be My messenger? Will you go to those who don't yet know Me, who haven't heard that there is a year of the Lord's favor and a new beginning? Do you want to be a kernel of wheat in My hand?" Are we quite certain that our answer was not just a cheap, "reasonable" or clever excuse to avoid God's calling? Are we certain that our present lives and our future plans are really God's will? Do they serve to make His mercy known in this world?

It is costly to be a kernel of wheat in God's hand. Our relationships constitute the first section of the field where we kernels are sowed in order to die, for God's kingdom is manifested there. When confronted with guilt and need, with rejection and pride, with mistrust and coldness; when we face the ugly, dark, painful part of most people's lives, we ourselves will die over and over again. But we can be certain that God will give over to death only the things which in any case cannot inherit His kingdom; they must be transformed by resurrection, which turns them into riches in God's kingdom.

If we do not evade this death we will be broken open like a kernel of wheat. This is not possible without our daily willingness to leave our secure homes and go out into the cold and danger; to fall down into the cold and vast waste of a field where we will have to give up what we have received: our safety and security. Our lives will seldom be spent in large amounts, but rather in small change. But without this daily dying the kingdom of God cannot attain life through us.

Day 124

WHOM SHALL I SEND?

Today half of the world's population is under fifteen years of age. It is distressing that so few accept the call to the Islamic world. It is equally grievous that so few women and even fewer men reach for children's hands to lead them out of a sea of misery, hopelessness and fear, so that they find a home with the heavenly Father and can set their feet on the rock of hope which is Jesus. Investing in children is clearly hard work for our hearts. It means losing our lives for their sakes so that they can experience God's fatherhood and motherhood in us. It is no small thing to lead children to God's fatherhood, to friendship and trust in Jesus.

The only path on which God comes to children and youth, on which He calls them to Himself, leads through our hearts. The price for this is calculated not only in the time, material things and emotional energy we must invest. The lion's share of the price we pay is our suffering that these children are in need and abandoned, which is usually the result of fatherlessness and even motherlessness.

When we devote ourselves to children we share their pain, their aggression, their powerlessness, as well as their loneliness and fear. Children are at the mercy of the world's dark powers, such as hatred, greed and apathy. Only genuine fathers and mothers can suffer with them. God is seeking men and women who will make His father- and

287

motherhood tangible and visible to these children and youth. Where are the witnesses? Where are the messengers? Where are the fathers? Where are the mothers?

Who is willing to renounce his professional, social, even his Christian career and give his life to children and youth in order to fulfill an ardent wish in God's heart? Without such dedication no new life will be born in these children; it will be almost impossible to lead them to the Father and help them achieve genuine personal development.

> "[U]nless a grain of wheat falls to the ground and dies, it remains only a single seed. But if it dies, it produces many seeds."
>
> (John 12:24)

This same principle applies to children and youth, whether in our own family or children in general. The children and youth of the world are waiting for us to give them our hearts and lead them to the Father in heaven. They need role models, friends, mothers and especially fathers in order to enter the kingdom of the heavenly Father. May this plea, which is God's plea, not leave our hearts untouched:

> Then I heard the voice of the Lord saying, "Whom shall I send? And who will go for us?"
>
> (Isaiah 6:8)

Section 15

SOWING WITH TEARS,
REAPING WITH JOY

When the Lord brought back the captives to
Zion, we were like men who dreamed.
Our mouths were filled with laughter,
our tongues with songs of joy.
Then it was said among the nations,
"The Lord has done great things for them."
The Lord has done great things for us,
and we are filled with joy.
Restore our fortunes, O Lord,
like streams in the Negev.
Those who sow in tears
will reap with songs of joy.
He who goes out weeping,
carrying seed to sow,
will return with songs of joy,
carrying sheaves with him.

(Psalm 126)

Day 125

TEARS ARE UNAVOIDABLE

In the book of Revelation we read,

"Now the dwelling of God is with men, and he will live with them. They will be his people, and God himself will be with them and be their God. He will wipe every tear from their eyes. There will be no more death or mourning or crying or pain, for the old order of things has passed away."

(21:3-4)

We find the same theme in the Old Testament, e.g. Isaiah 25:7-8,

On this mountain he will destroy
the shroud that enfolds all peoples,
the sheet that covers all nations;
he will swallow up death forever.
The Sovereign Lord will wipe away the tears from all faces;
he will remove the disgrace of his people from all the earth.

Have we ever wondered why both Isaiah and John speak of the day when God will wipe away all tears? It touched me to realize once again how much God wants to write on our hearts that a day will come when all tears will be wiped away – and He Himself will do it! This means that God is aware of tears.

Tears are an unavoidable reality, otherwise it would not be written that He will wipe away every tear from every face. Obviously tears are also part of our work in God's kingdom. But this is not what we expect. Who wants to get into situations which drive him to tears? This is not the future we are striving for. Everything the world undertakes is intended to avoid tears as far as possible. Our motto is fun, ease, recreation – but not tension and stress. It is an incredible promise that the day will come when God will wipe away all tears. What a future, that God Himself will wipe away the tears from each one of us! In other words, there will come a day of final and absolute comfort. When our tears are wiped away we are comforted. God says, "The time is coming when you will experience comfort in fullness."

Day 126

...LIKE MEN WHO DREAMED

Psalm 126 shows us that there is a home-coming. The day will come when we all return home. We are all waiting for this, longing for the day we finally arrive at the Father's home. We can't imagine how this will feel! The psalmist attempts to describe it. He says, "Our mouths will be filled with laughter," meaning that our whole being will be full of laughter. Everything inside us will break out into laughter when we are finally at home, yes, our whole being will break out in praise.

After having experienced the full impact of this revelation of coming home, the psalmist looks back and says of the path leading to this home, "Those who sow in tears will reap with songs of joy." These are tears which are sown. We cannot escape the reality that sowing has to do with tears, because sowing is strenuous and costs us a lot; it often wears us down and sometimes makes us sad as well. We weep from pain and disappointment, from grief and helplessness because we have reached the limits of our strength and abilities. As unpleasant as it may be for us, reaching our limits seems to be the only way we can grasp what God means when He says, "Not by might nor by power, but by my Spirit" (Zechariah 4:6).

Eternal fruit cannot grow through our efforts. We must reach the point where we throw ourselves totally and solely on God, so that He can cause the harvest to grow.

Day 127

GOD LETS US REACH OUR LIMITS

On our pathway through life, God does not protect us from reaching our limits. He does not protect us from experiencing our helplessness, nor from situations where we can do nothing but weep. Otherwise we would not read about tears. When we are serving Jesus, we often have the feeling that He should prepare a nice level path for us and remove every pebble. And because this is not the case, the enemy comes and says, "Can that be a path of life which leads us to our limits, which is filled with tears, helplessness, suffering and perseverance amidst tension?!"

We all reach our limits repeatedly. And the better we know ourselves, the more we realize how limited and narrow our heart is. The sooner we realize how terribly needy we are, the more we begin to suffer over ourselves. There is a great discrepancy between my heart knowledge of God and the reality of my relationship to Him. Recognizing this can cause us to cry, "Lord, help!"

When Paul had exactly this experience, he wrote, "What a wretched man I am! Who will rescue me...?" (Romans 7:24). He had seen what was really inside him and therefore lost every illusion about himself. Paul, a very gifted man who had achieved so much in God's kingdom, reached the point in life where he cried, "What a wretched man I am!"

This is the cry of one who has reached his limits. Paul weeps over himself because he has seen who he really is.

In our daily relationships, especially with those to whom we want to bring the gospel, we keep reaching our limits. We would prefer for everything to be easy – relaxed, without suffering, without disappointment. Therefore we are constantly looking for ways to make our life as free from pain and suffering as possible. And then we realize that it can't be done. If someone says he never reaches his limits, I doubt whether he is really spreading the gospel and has ever encountered sin in his own life and in others.

Day 128

ABRAHAM, A MODEL

When our experience drives us to tears and we're about to give up because it's so difficult, that's the best condition for sowing. And what is sowed? It is a sowing with the promise that there will be a joyful harvest. God does not want us to give up or shrink back. He wants us to begin sowing hope exactly at the point where we suffer over ourselves, where our inner narrowness is so obvious that it hurts and we have the feeling that no one can help us; where we say with Paul, "What a wretched man I am! There's no help for me." This is exactly the place where Jesus expects us to sow hope and to begin sowing His word into this reality.

What made the great men of the Bible into the models they are? For example, what made Abraham into a friend of God and a father of all who believe? If anyone was ever driven to tears, then it was Abraham. He had to lead his own son to the sacrificial altar – this beloved son whom he had longed for all his life and who, when he received him, embodied his future and his experience of God. I can imagine that Abraham died a thousand deaths. In such a situation, most of us would have said, "That's it. God can't expect this of me. I've had enough now." It would have been understandable if Abraham had reacted in this way. And as if this weren't enough, Isaac asked his father, "Where is the lamb?"

Overwhelming situations often confront us with very difficult questions. Abraham was not spared this either. And how did he respond? He made no excuses but sowed a seed of trust and hope which later bore fruit in the lives of Isaac and the whole people of Israel. For he said, "God himself will provide..." (Genesis 22:8). Abraham didn't understand what God was doing, but he confessed, "In this situation, which I don't understand, which is so unbearably painful, which brings me to my limits, I know one thing: God is here and He will take care of it. He will provide a lamb."

Day 129

SOWING TRUST AND HOPE

A man of God like Moses was also deeply disappointed after he had invested everything in the people of Israel and they had seen miracle after miracle. But as soon as he was absent for a few days, the people fell into deepest idolatry. Moses was shattered. Every one of us would have been. Even God said to Moses, "I understand you. Come, we'll stop trying with this people and I'll start over again with you!" Which one of us would not have said yes and would not have been honored that God wanted to begin a new generation with me!

Moses became a friend of God because at this point of deepest disappointment, where he reached his limits, he did not choose the easiest path, but said, "No, Lord, for Your sake I won't give up. For Your sake I'll continue with this people. What would people think of You? Lord, I don't want others to think evil of You and dishonor Your name" (see Exodus 32:1-14). Moses' awe of God was more important to him than his disappointment.

The men and women of God who bore fruit in His kingdom and set so much in motion were people whom God brought to their limits. They often wept – over man's spiritual need and hardened hearts, but over their own weaknesses as well. But in the midst of these difficulties they sowed trust and hope. Asaph wrote,

> Yet I am always with you; you hold me by my right hand...
> Whom have I in heaven but you?
>
> (Psalm 73:23, 25)

We usually can't see the connection between tears and God's special presence in our lives. But this is just the point – we are all on the way home, and it is a fact that on this path the two belong together. Whoever does not sow God's kingdom in the tears he sheds will not be able to reap. "He... goes out weeping, carrying seed to sow" (Psalm 126:6).

When we reach our limits, God doesn't hold it against us that we weep and struggle. But He does say, "Keep going, trust Me; sow hope, sow trust; give Me the honor; trust Me to reach the goal with you; trust Me to fulfill what I have planned; be quiet in this situation and wait for Me to intervene; don't start looking for your own solutions!" If we seek our own solutions we will reap only our own fruit. But God says, "If you sow trust in Me, I will let you reap My fruit. And this fruit will be joy." As we read in Psalm 126:6b, "He...will return with songs of joy, carrying sheaves with him."

Day 130

LAUGHTER WHICH FILLS
OUR WHOLE BEING

I want to encourage us regarding two things. First, when we reach our limits and are driven to tears we should not be dismayed and think something unusual is happening or that God is infinitely far away. And second, we should not wallow in complaints about God and other people, but realize that He is with us in the midst of everything. God is waiting for us to begin sowing by keeping on going and saying to Him, "Yet I am always with you. No matter what You allow, I know You are good. You will turn my situation around. I know You will take away my narrowness. You will lead me out into a wide place, as it is written, 'He brought me out into a spacious place; he rescued me because he delighted in me' (Psalm 18:19). I know that You will turn my inner desert into a blooming garden. I won't give up, no matter how many rocks I have to clear away from this garden. Lord, I won't give up because I know that after all the tears and struggles You will do what You said: You will wipe away all these tears and I will reap with joy."

What do we reap? We reap the experience of God's unspeakable presence. Is there anything more wonderful than standing in front of the Father and hearing Him say, "Now all suffering is ended." All problems, all struggles will come to an end. Even if it sounds like a dream, it is God's reality. And He wants to lead us into this reality, if we believe and trust Him.

Thank God that we do not have to wait for this comfort until we see Him face to face. God is so endlessly merciful that He gives us a taste of His comfort even now. But this taste cannot be compared to, nor is it even a glimmer of what God has ready for us. It is not just a sentimental wish, but God's reality. If we set our sights on this comfort and reaffirm daily, "Lord, I want to attain that," we will know that our tears are not the end. God's goal for us is joy, rejoicing and laughter which will fill our whole being.

IN THE FIERY OVEN OF LEUKEMIA

– A TESTIMONY BY REGULA REBIAI

I was thirty-five years old at the time, the mother of four children between five and twelve years, and together with my husband was responsible for a community of fifty adults and their children. For two years we and our family had lived in Jerusalem with some members of our community.

For several months I had felt very weak. I hadn't given it much thought – it just seemed a natural result of our challenging commission. I was often ill, which I attributed to the flu. But then more and more blue marks (haematomas) began to appear on my body, especially on my legs. My fatigue increased until coping with daily life took an enormous effort. Our family doctor in Switzerland advised me to have a blood test done. Almost all the results were abnormal. This was at the end of June, 1996. The family doctor referred me to a hematologist (blood specialist) in Israel for further tests.

The earliest available appointment with a specialist in the gigantic Hadassa Hospital in Jerusalem was 12 August, 1996. The hematologist immediately asked for a further test and, coming straight from the laboratory with the blood results in her hands, said, "Bad news, suspicion of leukemia (blood cancer). I have to admit you immediately." For my husband and me this was like a slap across the face! We hadn't expected this! We drove home, packed my things and prayed with the children. Friends stayed with them. At 8.00 p.m. we were back in the hospital. We couldn't comprehend it!

By the morning of 13 August there was a confirmed diagnosis of acute leukemia (AML). Many tests were carried out and in the evening I started a seven-day course of chemotherapy.

From one minute to the next it felt as if we were being confronted with one after another of the effects of this illness and with the prospect of death, and we were in deep shock. Our faith in the triune God and His Word suddenly became much more relevant. In this situation, could we say not only for ourselves but also for each of our four children, "we know that in all things God works for the good of those who love him" (Romans 8:28)? Faith that God would fulfill this word in us as well as in them, however He planned to do it, helped us overcome the initial shock. As inhuman, unnatural, irrational as it may appear, it can be God's best for the mother, for the children, for the father, and for everyone involved that a mother dies before she has finished bringing up her children. Then God Himself will have to fulfill His Word in all of them – and He is no man that He would lie…!

Chemotherapy

A week later, after completing the first course of chemotherapy, I was discharged from the hospital. On that day, there were two encouraging verses in our daily readings: "For he spoke and it came to be; he commanded, and it stood firm" (Psalm 33:9) and "Jesus called in a loud voice, 'Lazarus, come out!' The dead man came out" (John 11:43-44).

At first I had to go back to the hospital for check-ups every two days, then daily. I had to have many blood transfusions because my bone marrow had not returned to normal after the treatment, as hoped. The level of cancer cells in the blood was still over 50 per cent.

On 8 September I was hospitalized again in Jerusalem for a second course of chemotherapy. This time the dose was twenty times higher than the first course, because the doctors wanted to destroy the cancer cells completely. This strong medication robbed me of all my physical strength and for several days I lay lifelessly in bed as if I were weighed down with heavy stones. I was also suffering from a very itchy rash over my whole body and nausea. My blood count plummeted again, the bone marrow was destroyed and my immune system was almost nonexistent. In order to avert an infection I was given several antibiotics every day. Anxious days of hope followed: would my bone marrow ever recover and begin making blood again?!

After twenty-eight days, I was transferred to Switzerland because of our health insurance. Marcel and the children had already been there on furlough for several days.

The bone marrow test in mid-October showed a 95 per cent remission – that is, less than 5 per cent of the bone marrow blood cells were assumed to be still cancer cells, as they were not clearly identifiable in the test. A very positive improvement which we saw as a visible expression of God's intervention! Thanks to these good results and because the family was in Switzerland only for a limited time, the doctors waited before beginning a third and final course of chemotherapy and I was released from hospital for several days.

On 29 October the third course of chemotherapy began in Zurich. This was intended to stabilize the condition of my bone marrow. This course also lasted for five days and when my blood status collapsed, I again became dependent on intravenous antibiotics. For days I lay in bed without strength – this time I remained in hospital for thirty-six days! After this third treatment the bone marrow recovered very slowly. The strong regimen had taken a heavy toll on my inner organs. The liver values were too high, my

305

digestion hardly functioned and I was in constant danger of contracting an infection or of uncontrollable bleeding. And yet there were no hemorrhages or other complications which can keep a patient in hospital for weeks or even months after chemotherapy or can even prove fatal! Apart from the fact that I lost my hair, my body was not outwardly affected. I was even able to maintain my weight.

Struggle for trust

When I first heard the diagnosis "acute leukemia," it was a tremendous blow. The evil one whispered to me, "Now I have you and I'll kill you! I'll destroy all your plans and God's plans for your life!" Could it be, after all, that the evil one is stronger than God? Could it be that he really can do with me what he wants and I'm at his mercy, without defense?! The only thing I knew about leukemia was that you die of it... I sensed clearly that I now had to decide: Whom would I believe? Is it really true that for those who love God all things work together for good?! Is that also true now, in our situation?!

Right from that first day, while we were driving home to pack my things for hospital, I decided to turn wholly to God, to trust Him, to expect everything of Him and not close myself to His unfathomable working. Like the three friends in the fiery furnace I decided to say,

> "If we are thrown into the blazing furnace, the God we serve is able to save us from it, and he will rescue us from your hand, O king. But even if he does not, we want you to know, O king, that we will not serve your gods or worship the image of gold you have set up."
>
> (Daniel 3:17-18)

I made this decision right at the very beginning and I returned to it over and over again. I wanted to continue to say from my whole heart, "Great and marvelous are your deeds, Lord God Almighty. Just and true are your ways, King of the ages" (Revelation 15:3b). We had just recently set this verse at the head of our prayer letter. And now I had to really learn to take it literally. With all my strength I hung onto God and His Word, in order to honor Him in everything and not distance myself from Him.

How often in our community worship had I prayed this prayer of Charles de Foucauld:

My father,
I give myself to you,
Do whatever you want with me.
Whatever you want to do with me, I thank you.

I am ready for everything, I accept everything.
If only your will is fulfilled in me
And in all your creatures,
Then I long for nothing further, my God.

I lay my soul in your hands;
I give it to you, my God
With all the love of my heart, because I love you
And because this love drives me

To give myself to you,
To lay myself in your hands,
Without measure, with unlimited trust.
For you are my father!

With all the determination I could muster I wanted to continue to pray this prayer and completely relax in God's hands. I struggled for this total trust in God and His

307

working. Not necessarily that He would heal me, but that He would in fact make this present situation and everything coming of it turn out for the best for everyone. I did not fight for my life, because I am not afraid of dying. But I found the thought of leaving the children and Marcel, of not being able to finish raising the children and of leaving Marcel alone with this task very painful.

No stroke of fate

From the beginning I was aware of the fact that it was no stroke of fate that this illness had hit me. It was not just my or our problem how we would get through this difficult period. With this problem, God had placed Himself in the center not only of our lives but also of all our friends' lives. Suddenly He was being talked about, even by those who otherwise had no time for Him. "God, why are You allowing this?!"

What I can say is that deep down I realized in a new way that my life is in God's hand. It is in God's hand when I am healthy just as when I have the flu, am involved in an accident, war breaks out, or a terminal illness is diagnosed. Whatever happens I am in God's hand in exactly the same way. And what more can I wish for?! Does that make me afraid or relaxed? That depends on the kind of relationship I have to God, on what kind of God I turn to...

Taken out

For us as people who value relationships, fellowship and family life so highly, this time of illness and the separation it caused brought much tension and pain. The most painful thing for me was that I was unable to be a mother to our children in the way I had been accustomed to. I simply had to leave almost everything to others. At the same time, I was privileged, as it was not just anyone who took over my duties, but fellow believers from our community who knew our children well.

What comforted and often calmed me in this situation was the fact that my husband Marcel stepped into the missing motherly role. He cared for the children more than ever – and that in addition to his already overly full schedule! He practiced Hebrew with Immanuel, prepared Ephraim for his French exam, went for a walk with Hanna, helped Elija practice viola, took all the children to their annual dental check-ups, looked after all their hundred little problems and much more – all the things a mother does all day in addition to the cleaning and ironing.

We asked ourselves over and over again, "How can we maintain family life in this situation?" When I had enough strength, the children visited me one at a time in the hospital; they talked a lot and asked many things (especially about the illness), or we played together. I told stories and did crafts with Hanna and Immanuel. Sometimes we were also together as a whole family. We played in one of the empty hospital rooms and ate a snack or supper together. To God's glory we can say that the children did not become insecure. Despite all the pain and privations, their relationship to God and to us carried them through.

I was torn out of my leadership responsibilities. I had already been in the process of handing some of these areas over to others, which made it easier for me to let go.

But I was also cut off from the community. I could no longer eat with them, share, worship, take the Lord's Supper, celebrate the feasts... One day I wrote in my diary, "I'm involuntarily isolated, eat alone, sleep alone, read alone – I'm always alone except when someone visits; but that's so artificial, not real life..."

In fact I had a lot of time for myself – an unusual situation for a mother of four children! When I had enough strength, I used these times primarily to be with God.

Man does not live by bread alone...

I held fast to God's Word. It became my daily bread, giving my thoughts direction, calming my upset emotions and bringing God's realities close. I read much and often in His Word; everything else lost power and meaning for me and became secondary. God's Word sprang to life for me; every verse spoke to me quite personally. I experienced that God's Word really is full of life; it is powerful and sharper than any double-edged sword so that it penetrates and divides between soul and spirit; it judges thoughts and attitudes of the heart (cf. Hebrews 4:12). I could fully identify with many of the psalmists' experiences; from the depths of my heart I could pray their prayers, complain with them and cry out with them. God alone became important. It was just as Blaise Pascal had once formulated in a prayer:

> *To whom shall I call, LORD, if not to you?*
> *For nothing and no one except God can fulfill my hope.*
> *You alone were able to create my soul.*
> *You alone can create it anew and impress on it the image of*
> *your holy Son, my Savior.*

I had much time to talk to Jesus, to ask Him questions, to see, to experience. It was an intensive time of encountering God, during which I was able to experience His affection and care for me. Day and night I was aware of my bond with God. It seemed to me as if I were always standing before His throne.

Free to witness

Deep in my heart I began to comprehend more and more that God would keep His Word. I became certain that Romans 8:28 must be true, that "in all things God works for the good of those who love him." Even though I could not understand or explain everything, God does not speak empty words. His word is power and life. The peace of God came. This total trust in God, in His working and in His love to me, became my most precious possession.

With this, fear also disappeared. I became free to turn again to others, beginning with Marcel and the children. I became interested again in what Marcel was doing and thought it through with him. I was concerned about our children, where they stood, what they needed, how I could be a mother to them even within this limited framework. I turned again to my fellow believers from the community as well, supporting them in my thoughts and prayers.

I also became concerned about the nurses and doctors whom I saw so many times during the course of the day and, because my fear was gone, I became free to tell them about my living God. I developed personal relationships with many of them. They told me about themselves, asked questions about life, and repeatedly we talked about God – who He is and what He has to do with us. Even without mentioning God, they sensed His presence with me, they smelled the fragrance of true life. They mentioned this over and over again and they enjoyed coming to my room because there was peace and security here.

Thus, even in my greatest weakness, when I didn't know what was going to happen to me, I could again place myself at God's disposal. That gave me great joy, because I love to talk to people about Jesus.

God speaks about healing

Quite early on in my first stay in hospital Jesus said to me, "Now turn again to life. It is not yet time to die. When it is time, I will tell you." I had thought so intensively about my death that these words surprised me. Was that really Jesus' voice – or was it my own desires speaking?! I asked Jesus. And He replied, "My sheep hear My voice. You belong to My sheep."

Gradually Jesus began to speak about healing, too. He spoke to me through His Word, but also through many other believers. We held fast to these words in hope, knowing that we cannot and do not want to demand anything of God. When the prognosis from the doctors seemed quite bleak, when I had another infection and high fever, when I was in danger of death, I again fought the great battle of thoughts. "Did God really say that you will recover?! Do you really believe that?! There isn't really a chance, don't you see that? It's hopeless. Give up." I often felt attacked by the evil one and in my physical and emotional weakness I didn't have many resources with which to resist. Some days the battle was intense and I had only one thought: to remain with God, no matter what happened.

We were grateful for the doctors' efforts and the medical possibilities as an instrument in God's hand. And yet my life did not depend on the medical efforts, as difficult as that was for my human heart to comprehend. If God wanted me to live, then I would live. If God did not want me to, then no doctor could help me either. God alone has the right to bring my life to a conclusion, whenever He wants to. My life is in His hand, in no other.

Healed

After the third course of chemotherapy, a test showed that my bone marrow had returned to normal. The type of leukemia I had, if treated with chemotherapy only (without a bone marrow transplant), has statistically a 20 per cent chance of healing. The doctors were therefore recommending a bone marrow transplant, if a suitable donor could be found. This would have meant several months in hospital, including weeks of isolation – a great torture, physically and emotionally. In my case, such a transplant would have been very risky (sudden death), but the chances of recovery would have risen to 40 per cent.

But we did not have the impression from God that I should have a transplant and turned it down. We had no reason to believe that I was not among this 20 per cent. We believed that I was healed, even if no one could prove it. Here again I needed to believe that "my times are in your hands" (Psalm 31:15).

I was discharged from hospital. During the following weeks and months I had to have regular blood tests, which indicated a balanced blood count each time. I needed no further medication. But it took a year before my body functioned fully normally again. I became tired quickly, long evenings were strenuous and I had little stamina. But otherwise I was fully well and my life was in no way limited!

Jesus gave me a second life, we are very much aware of that! That is a great gift. And more than before I wanted to live only for Him. It is just as Paul said, "If we live, we live to the Lord; and if we die, we die to the Lord" (Romans 14:8).

Grace: God came to my aid...

During this time of illness I became acquainted with God's grace in a new way. During my whole struggle to trust Him He repeatedly came toward me. He never left me sitting in my own incapacity to take steps of faith. He didn't simply make demands ("Trust Me!") and then wait until I fulfilled them. Many times He reminded me of His words to me and led my thoughts back to Himself. When I called to Him for help, He came and helped me. He cared for me as a father cares for all the large and small things which concern his child.

...Through Marcel

God helped me especially through Marcel, my husband. Again and again I experienced Jesus coming close to me in Marcel, speaking to me and encouraging me. During this time of weakness and great tension, it was liberating and comforting to be under Marcel's spiritual protection and to be covered by him. I could tell him about all my questions and what attacks and doubts I was experiencing. It was never too much for him, even when I fell into the same doubts over and over again. I could entrust myself wholly to him and needed to cover up neither my weakness nor my nakedness. When I lost my vision and was discouraged, he helped me order my thoughts and turn to God again.

...Through my brothers and sisters

Our community members were also a great help and encouragement. They created space for us and were always ready to help. That took a great deal of pressure away from us and helped us maintain our family framework. They stood before God with me during this time. In Israel's hospitals, the medical standard is high, but the care is quite rudimentary. Therefore every day someone from the community visited me to bring tea, make a hot water bottle, remake the bed, etc. I was grateful that once a day I did not have to eat alone, that we could pray together and share.

And now?

My body needed about a year to recover from the exertion and the effects of the strong chemotherapy. My blood count remained normal and I needed no further medication. My soul and my inner life needed more time in order to find their way back to the world of the living and to fully participate in the hustle and bustle of life. But life also became much more precious to me. I was much more aware of the uniqueness of each moment and of the gift of relationships; I could enjoy this but also take responsibility. At the same time, life became less important because in my own body I had experienced the temporariness and the limits of our earthly life.

In the years since my illness God has blessed me with great energy, perhaps even greater and more clearly targeted than before my illness. I can invest this energy in my family, in our community and in a great number of other people.

I only recently realized just how great the miracle of my healing was when the doctor who had treated me in Zurich told me that I had only had a 2 per cent chance of recovery.

No wonder the doctors in Jerusalem had considered me a hopeless case!

As challenging, painful and difficult as this time was, the resulting fruit for us and for many others has been incredibly valuable. The illness forced us to define what is truly essential in our lives and, with God's help and mercy, to concentrate on what we discovered to be the one important thing in life: no matter what God does, He is good and His ways are just! We were determined to be faithful to Him in everything, even if this meant letting go of life.

We knew we had to live in the knowledge that being intact and healthy cannot be our life goal, in comparison with eternal life, because everyone must die. We wanted to hold fast to our firm trust and faithfulness toward God because this relationship will remain in eternity. We wanted to make this concrete not just for ourselves but also teach it to our children.

The foundation which God built during the time of pain, pressure and confrontation with illness and death has become a great blessing to us in the past years. In many a tense situation we can confidently remain firm, without fear, distrust or accusation toward God, but in the deep certainty that He leads on paths to life. God has eternity in mind, not just our momentary needs! Thus Psalm 116 became an important prayer for me during my illness – and it still is today:

> I love the Lord, for he heard my voice;
> he heard my cry for mercy.
> Because he turned his ear to me,
> I will call on him as long as I live.
> The cords of death entangled me,
> the anguish of the grave came upon me;
> I was overcome by trouble and sorrow.
> Then I called on the name of the Lord: "O Lord, save me!"

The Lord is gracious and righteous;
our God is full of compassion.
The Lord protects the simple-hearted;
when I was in great need, he saved me.
Be at rest once more, O my soul,
for the Lord has been good to you.
For you, O Lord, have delivered my soul from death,
my eyes from tears, my feet from stumbling,
that I may walk before the Lord in the land of the living.
I believed; therefore I said, "I am greatly afflicted."
And in my dismay I said, "All men are liars."
How can I repay the Lord for all his goodness to me?
I will lift up the cup of salvation
and call on the name of the Lord.
I will fulfill my vows to the Lord
in the presence of all his people.
Precious in the sight of the Lord is the death of his saints.
O Lord, truly I am your servant;
I am your servant, the son of your maidservant;
you have freed me from my chains.
I will sacrifice a thank-offering to you
and call on the name of the Lord.
I will fulfill my vows to the Lord
in the presence of all his people,
in the courts of the house of the Lord –
in your midst, O Jerusalem.
Praise the Lord.

ABOUT THE AUTHOR

Marcel Rebiai was born in Algeria and grew up in Switzerland with foster parents. He trained as a primary teacher and as a state church youth worker.

He is the founder and leader of the Community of Reconciliation which is based in Jerusalem. He is married to Regula, with four children and an adopted son. He is the author of *Islam, Israel and the Church* and has an international teaching ministry.

The Community of Reconciliation works among Jews and Moslems in Israel and France. Their efforts concentrate on:

- general reconciliation ministry based on the gospel of Jesus, the Messiah

- reconciliation between Jews and Arabs, as well as between Israel and the nations

- community living; prayer; proclaiming the good news of Jesus Christ through friendships and an authentic lifestyle.

For further information or to order the quarterly COR publications (available in English) please contact:

GDV-COR office
PO Box 77
CH-8625 Gossau ZH
Switzerland
office@gdv-cor.org
www.gdv-cor.ch

We hope you enjoyed reading this
Sovereign World book.
For more details of other Sovereign
books and new releases see our website:

www.sovereignworld.com

You can also join us on Facebook and Twitter.

If you would like to help us send a copy of
this book and many other titles to needy
pastors in developing countries, please
write for further information or send your
gift to:

Sovereign World Trust
PO Box 777
Tonbridge, Kent TN11 0ZS
United Kingdom

www.sovereignworldtrust.com

The Sovereign World Trust
is a registered charity.